Table of Contents

Rise and Fall of the Indignants-Aganaktismenoi

Historical Context

Introduction

The aim of this book is to give a flavour to the English speaking world of the situation in Greece under the iron heel of the EU and the IMF. Not a day passes without mention of Greece in the worlds mass media of disinformation. It's as if original sin has been replaced with everything that is reported from Greece. At the same time this book documents an extremely small amount of what has been occurring via the medium of eyewitness reports and aims to highlight the despicable role of the official Left mis-leaderships who have left opportunity after opportunity slide. Instead of starting from events, mass de-industrialisation, mass sustained illegal immigration, mass unemployment and rampant inflation they have assumed like an ostrich that if they wish the capitalist crisis away, it will go. As such they have been totally and abysmally unprepared on a scale not seen since Germany in the 1920's. They have refused to call joint coordinated sustained strike action, they have refused to support strikes held by sections of Greeks they don't influence like the Hauliers or the Taxi-Drivers instead preferring 24 hour union parades. They refused to support and promote the rise of the Greek Indignados and their abstentionist politics from the social battles Greeks are forced into does, not reach Parliament where they have steadfastly refused to leave even when its role is now defunct as decisions are clearly taken solely in Brussels and Washington.

The real drama is yet to unfold and as such this small contribution is dedicated to all those comrades I have known personally over the years in going back and forth to Greece and my opinions are flavoured by their invaluable contributions with which none of this would have been possible. In the not too distant future the hope is that a real Left will be reborn from the ashes of the old and able to directly confront the dying beast that is global capitalism. Until that day more tragedies await us…

VN Gelis
London
4th October 2011

Arrival of the IMF

Editor's Note: It has now been revealed that the data used for Greece to join both the Euro and then the IMF weren't really held up to public scrutiny. This series of articles try to analyse the role of Greek capitalism leading up to the arrival of the IMF and the disaster that was about to be unleashed on the Greek people.

ASOK (Pan-Hellenic Socialist Movement) George Papandreou, and recently elected prime minister announced that Greece's public finances were much worse than he expected.

Six months later he announced that in order to balance the budget it was necessary to embrace an austerity programme drawn up in collaboration with the IMF and the EU. Yet as recently as March this year the IMF chief, Strauss Kahn declared Greece didn't require a bailout. Yet now we have lived through the biggest EU "bailout" in history; how did it come to this?

Thirty years membership of the European Union has brought Greece to the verge of economic collapse. A predominantly agricultural producer it never industrialised to the extent of the northern countries of the EU as during the 19th century Greece itself was a colony of the Ottoman Empire and after 'liberation' after 1918 was under the joint supervision of France, Britain and Russia.

After the Second World War the EU was sold to the Greek people as a way of the country being developed. Instead the exact opposite has occurred, irrespective of the fact that certain infrastructure projects have occurred during this period – including airports, roads and telecommunications.

Having medium-sized heavy industries predominantly in shipping repairs, bus manufacturing and solar panels it has lost almost all its manufacturing in a de-industrialisation frenzy that would make Thatcher proud. Globalisation has brought it to its knees as almost all the shipping crews of one of the world's largest shipping fleets replaced their crews in the 1970s with lower paid labour from third world countries like the Philippines.

Agriculture and the EU were sold to the Greek people as the path along which Greek producers would increase their exports; but instead via the domination of the supply chain by multinational supermarkets, non-EU imports have increased exponentially to the detriment of Greek produce.

The crippling forest fires and the destruction of olive trees, as well as the heat waves of the last few years, have meant agriculture is on the verge of meltdown. For the last 20 years the sector is staffed by workers who live in huts with the animals and are paid third-world subsistence wages. Agriculture now constitutes a very small percentage of GDP around 8%, unlike the 1970s when it was around 28%.

The mass building boom in holiday flats led to huge oversupply; thousands of properties remain unsold and building activity has dropped by 45% since the credit crunch. Historically the building workers in the 1960s and 1970s were the wage setters for the whole of the labour movement but their union organisation was broken in the early 1990s and the workforce was replaced on the whole by cheap immigrant labour, initially from neighbouring countries.

Average wages are about €50 a day for more than eight-hours work. Insurance cover is non-existent and health and safety measures rarely count. The 2004 Olympics "boom" led to many building workers' deaths and hundreds of millions spent on infrastructure which for the most part is now rotting or has been handed over to ship-owners for free.

Health and education sectors have not fared much better. Whilst an "NHS" was created in the 1980s successive cost reductions over the last decade (due to syphoning money off to pay for the Olympics and arms budgets) many Greek islands no longer have national hospital facilities and people die on the way or while waiting for helicopters to take them off. Doctors only function with a "bribe" – a way of aiding their exceptionally low average government salaries.

Educational provision has expanded with many universities having been built (16 in total) but without basic infrastructure linked to them. Universities in name they exist to mask the dreadful youth unemployment figures which hover around the 20-40% mark. Unable to get decent jobs many are forced to live with their parents throughout their 20s and 30s.

Most of the secondary schools in the Athens regions continue to have two shifts as there is not enough class room space to handle the volume of pupils. Pupils spend most of their time either at school or in night classes which they have to pay for to cover the course work they were supposed to have done in the day; it is the only way of having a realistic chance of passing the exams.

Insofar as job opportunities and conditions were constantly deteriorating in the private sector, people sought refuge in the public sector. That kept the working poor afloat, since if one person in a family had someone working for the government then the family could survive. But in the last few years the privatisation of OTE-Telecommunications, Olympic Airways, together with the subcontracting of many public sector posts in the railways, post-offices, water company etc., many Greeks were offered part-time posts on different rates of pay to the full-timers as well as some doing fulltime work on part-time rates.

Role of the Left

The Greek TUC (GSEE) and the ADEDY (public sector workers' union) have traditionally been PASOK fiefdoms with the leaders appointed by PASOK. Often, after being a leader of GSEE or ADEDY then one "graduates" to becomes a PASOK MP.

The other union federation is PAME – belonging to the Stalinist KKE party. It split from GSEE a few years ago, claiming it is building class struggle union. In the last six months they say they have got the majority of 85 union federations on their side and the demonstration on 15 May – where about 200,000 took part – certainly backed this up. Both Federations have called a series of 24-hour strikes, sometimes extending for as long as 48-hours.

The austerity packages

The measures announced have included basic across-the-board pay cuts of about 10% and pension entitlement reductions. These have been pushed through at the same time as petrol prices have soared 100% in a few months, prices of basic foodstuffs have risen by anything between 10-20% and unemployment is skyrocketing as many small businesses are going out of businesses.

Basic pensions for those who have contributed to them are about €500-700 euros a month; those who haven't paid in contributions receive about €300euros but without a contribution to their housing costs. Unemployment pay only exists for those who have contributed at least a year and then it only lasts for six months, so many bosses hire people then sack them, as they know they will get money from the state and the bosses a subsidy if they take on people sent from the dole office. So long term work has become a thing of the past or only for those who still have state jobs.

The fight back

Once the measures were announced a very large demo – on a scale not seen since the pension battle of 2001 – of around 250,000 people congregated outside parliament in Athens. It was to be a typical demo of the unions whereby the GSEE members would meet in one square (Sintagma) and march to another (Omonia) while the PAME-KKE contingents would do exactly the reverse.

The General Strike of 5-6 May, however, didn't take the normal course of events of marching from a to b, listening to the standard rhetorical speeches promising militancy in the future, but not here and now. The police didn't expect the KKE-PAME ranks to become uncontrollable as they have strong stewards, but the ranks of working class people who happened to be on the demo far outnumbered the organised columns of the KKE-PAME.

People showed a determination and a willingness to encircle parliament even to break through inside and not allow the politicians to leave. Individual workers shouted very militant slogans about "hanging traitors and burning down parliament". Some workers confronted the police individually with a determination not seen for many years.

Whilst these developments were occurring something else was happening in another part of town. A bank, belonging to the businessman who bought out Olympic Airways, was allegedly burnt down by anarchists. Three bank workers were burnt to death. This event was used as an excuse by the KKE-PAME to ask people to dissolve and go home after they were tear gassed by the police on the steps of parliament.

The day after the KKE announced that those who tried to storm parliament were the Greek equivalent of the fascist BNP and "provocateurs", language quite familiar to the KKE's pro-establishment history from the murder of their guerrilla leader Velouhiotis during World War Two, to the student killed in the July days of the 1960's Petrula, to the occupation of the Polytechnic on 17 November 1973 which triggered the fall of the junta.

So, despite having gained a majority in the unions and having impressive numbers at their command, the KKE only continued the policies of GSEE – calling 24-hour token protests. Every opportunity was squandered or demobilized on the pretext of their being a provocation led by ...extremists.

Parliament passes the attacks

A week later the austerity measures were voted for by the Greek parliament During the evening the KKE deliberately marched from Sintagma square (where parliament is) to Omonia and the GSEE marched the other way with the ex-eurostalinists and other leftists behind them

(SIRIZA (Eurostalinists) and NAR, EEK, SWP gathered under the organisational framework of Antarsya).

Whilst this time 30,000 refused to leave parliament and wanted to block the MPs' exit the left put down their banners and asked via their loudhailers for the people to go home – thus adopting the policies of the KKE which they are allegedly against. The hundreds of thousands willing to fight that day found no leadership worthy of the name, just endless speeches about how the measures will be beaten in the future.

Despite having been offered loans at 1% by both the Russia and China, Papandreou is dead set on implementing the wishes and desires of the hedge funds. No doubt when his job here is done he will relocate to Switzerland or New York to work for them. The hope is that his exit from government will be provoked by some spark that will truly light a fire and he will suffer the same fate as some Latin American politicians who in the space of hours ended up in private jets trying to get out of their country after a mass rebellion.

For Greece to survive even in the short term, it has to abandon the Euro, try to control imports in particular agricultural ones, cancel all the foreign debts and embark on a programme of nationalisation without compensation of the major industries and banks. It should stop paying €7bn annually to European arms' manufacturers and demand restitution for all damage inflicted on the economy from WW2. Without a militant fighting programme that doesn't limit itself to 24 and 48-hour token protests there will be no hope within the EU.

The first signs of this starting are two events. PASOK politicians have been reported to have been abused in public and women have started a protest in Thessalonica banging their cooking pots demanding food Argentinian style. Let us work for a movement such as rocked that country in 2001-2002.

Thu 20, May 2010 @ 10:19

VNGelis said…

Another 24hour general strike occurred today and the KKE-Communist Party excelled itself in its sectarian divisive action propping up Papandreou's government. Instead of marching from Sintagma (Parliament Sq. to Omonia) they marched from Omonia to the Ministry of Labour and then asked its people to disperse walking to Thiseo, the area around the Akropolis which is in the EXACT opposite direction of Parliament... Stalinists see Parliament now like the Dracula sees the cross, they avoid it at all costs as the most impoverished gather there who want the struggle to continue in a militant fashion.

GSEE-TUC with the Eurostalinists Siriza and the leftists of Antarsya marched to Parliament but ensured they continued past it in a rush refusing to congregate there. Thousands remained outside shouting militant slogans:

'Thieves Thieves'

'Scumbags, Traitors, Politicians'

'Send PM George to Goudi (Prison)'

'Take your mother and leave the People don't Want You'

'Unions which overthrow not Submit',

'Here and Now Cancel all Foreign Debts',

'Bread, Education, Freedom, the Junta never died in 1973'

'Send Jeffrey (PM George's nickname) to the USA'

To the police a section of the demonstrators chanted 'It will become like Argentina', 'Guard those that rob you', 'Shameless drop down your shields'

When the demo passed outside the Marfin Bank 'Chrisohoidi, (Minister of the Interior) Provocateur, Murderer'

These 24hour token strikes are reaching their historical limits. There is no point in marching 6-8 times to Parliament or from Parliament to fight another day. The leaders of the official left despite the numbers of people involved are working in tandem trying to weaken the resistance and peoples resolve. The economic crisis is becoming clearly a crisis of leadership as the measures aren't going away but will get worse as cuts have now been extended to the private sector, not just the public sector workers according to the latest info from the IMF.

Thu 20, May 2010 @ 23:12

On the Death of Marfin Bank Employees...

VNGelis said...

The management of the bank strictly bared the employees from leaving today, even though they had persistently asked so themselves from very early this morning – while they also forced the employees to lock up the doors and repeatedly confirmed that the building remained locked up throughout the day, over the phone. They even blocked off their internet access so as to prevent the employees from communicating with the outside world.

Employee

Whilst the disturbances were occurring BBC news networks which the only one was showing the disturbances went down. In particular the section of the demo which moved to occupy Parliament. The Greek media was on strike for the whole day.

After about an hour CNN announces first 3 people have died from a bank fire to the world. Then the Greek media starts to work again, the 3 dead dominate the news and newspapers are printed for next day despite a 48hour strike. Taking into account that Vgenopoulos was handed Olympic Airways on a plate in a rigged privatisation process and a section of the redundant workers attacked the leaders of the Greek TUC in a public demo for selling them out, it isn't beyond the pale to assume this was an inside job.

Fri 07, May 2010 @ 09:34

The International Journal of INCLUSIVE DEMOCRACY, Vol. 5, No. 4 / Vol. 6, No. 1 (Autumn 2009 / Winter 2010)

Greece: The implosion of the systemic crisis

TAKIS FOTOPOULOS

Greece has been again front-page news in the world press in the last few months.

First, because of the new flare-up of riots in Athens in December 2009 caused by the alienated youth of the country marking the first anniversary of the police killing of a 15-year old student a year before —when an unprecedented social explosion took place, which, as I tried to show a few months ago, [1] had not been seen again since the student uprising in the early seventies that eventually led to the fall of the military junta in 1974. However, this was only a pretext and the new flare-up should be seen, in fact, as part of a process indicating the flimsy foundations on which the post-war social and economic system has been built and, also, as an indication of the fact that the systemic crisis in Greece is continuously deepening. In this context, the recent Greek elections in October, which gave an overwhelming parliamentary majority to PASOK's social-liberals and was celebrated by the political and economic elites both in Greece and abroad, could be shown to be just a sideshow, mostly irrelevant to the underlying social processes going on, their only real interest being that they were indicative of the elites' plans for the future.

Second, because of the near bankruptcy of the Greek economy when it was revealed that it enjoyed the highest combination of public debt and budget deficit as a proportion to GDP among the Eurozone countries. This prompted the rating agencies to downgrade Greece as regards the degree of reliability in repaying its huge debts to foreign lenders, boosting the "spreads" (i.e. the rate at which the Greek state could borrow compared to Germany) to a record level and creating a vicious circle as regards the financial reliability of the Greek elites, while giving at the same time the chance to the European elites to impose almost unbearable conditions on the Greek people, in order to continue lending the Greek elites —perpetuating in the process the economic and political dependence of the country on them! The outcome, as usual in these cases, is that the Greek people and particularly the lower social strata would be called upon to pay the heavy price of further borrowing, (in terms of lower incomes and employment), so that the local and foreign elites could continue enjoying their huge income and wealth which they have accumulated.

In this article, I will examine, first, the political bankruptcy in connection to the October elections and recent events, and I will discuss next the present near economic bankruptcy in relation to the myth of "green growth" promoted by the reformist Left and Greens and, after I consider the social crisis with reference to the systemic problem of immigration, I will continue on with the massive suppression of the December demonstrations, which confirmed the rise of social-fascism in Greece. Finally, I will examine the current attempt by the EU elites to transform Greece into an EU protectorate and I will propose an alternative solution that will aim to stop the Latin-Americanisation of Greece, and create the preconditions for a self-reliant economic democracy as an integral part of on an Inclusive Democracy.

Political bankruptcy, elections and parliamentary parties

It is now clear that the decision to call a general election, just two years after the previous one, was very much enforced on the political elites by the local economic elites and the EU elites, in view of the social unrest that would inevitably have followed the introduction by a right-wing government of the radical reforms of "structural adjustment" demanded by the EU and other international organizations (OECD, IMF etc.). Particularly so, as these reforms would inevitably have included drastic restrictions on public spending (health, social security, etc.), suppression of wages and pensions, further "flexibility" of labour and so on, aiming at a drastic improvement of the competitiveness of the public and private sectors at the expense of the working people, in other words, aiming at the completion of the country's economic integration into neoliberal globalisation. Of course, whether the political and economic elites and the new government which expresses their interests will manage at the end to avoid an effective systemic (economic and political) bankruptcy is another story, which will be determined by the outcome of the social struggle, now reaching a critical turning point.

However, given the above plans of the European and local elites, it is not surprising that the overwhelming victory of the social-liberal PASOK party in the October general election was celebrated by the elites, locally and abroad. This is particularly so, after the December 2008 social explosion made clear the extent of the systemic crisis in Greece. It was at this particular point that the elites realised that the need for a self-declared "socialist" government to take over, with the main aim to introduce the drastic "reforms" mentioned above, was imperative.

PASOK —today under the leadership of George Papandreou (offspring of the Papandreou dynasty of the centre-"Left") was the "perfect" choice for the elites, as this party has governed Greece, in turns with the Karamanlis dynasty of the centre-Right, during the entire post-junta period that followed the fall of the military dictatorship in 1974. In fact, these two dynasties, initially under the tutelage of the British and then of the US elite, and, lately, under that of the transnational elite, have been the main players of the Greek political scene for the entire post-war period, which began with the end of the Greek Civil War in the late 1940's. However, the very fact that PASOK managed to gain a comfortable parliamentary majority (thanks to an electoral system that blatantly favours the first party in number of votes), in reality, sowed winds which, most likely, will, soon, reap whirlwinds. This is because the bipartisan system in Greece is not based on any solid foundations. An indication of this is the fact that, while in Europe, neo-liberal parties alternate with social-liberal ones (which have, long ago, abandoned even the socialist rhetoric) on the basis of a clear agenda that summarises the demands of neo-liberal globalisation, in Greece, both parties, and especially the social-liberals, systematically hide their true identity! When therefore, the true identity of PASOK is being revealed today, following the harsh measures it is introducing to deal with the crisis, its electoral base is in fact being dismantled and the result may well be the future dissolution not just of PASOK but of the entire bipartisan system in Greece.

It is clear that the same, more or less policies, with perhaps small variations on the actual fiscal measures to be introduced, would have been adopted by whatever party was elected, given the main goal imposed by the European Monetary Union (EMU) on all member-states for the reduction of the public debt to meet the Maastricht Treaty criteria. The "choice" given by the elites to the Greek people was clear: either to re-elect the previous governing party (New Democracy) with an explicit new mandate to implement the savage cuts in social spending suggested by the EU commission and international organisations, or to elect a party (PASOK) which was in fact deceiving the electorate that it could somehow avoid the suggested savage cuts —in other words, a party that was, in fact, relying on its socialist name and its control of trade union bureaucracies to pass exactly the same policies! The method has been, after all, successfully tested for many years by the British Labour party, with the full support of the elites in Britain. It is therefore obvious that PASOK aspires to play exactly the same role now, with the full support of the local elites, which played a crucial role in its rise to power.

As for the New Democracy Party, it was apparently "sacrificed" temporarily by the economic and political elites in the EU and Greece, on the expectation that a "socialist" government could pass the same measures much easier, given its control of trade union leaderships. So, the only hope of its newly elected leadership for a return to power —in case PASOK is finally dismantled following its present irreparable damage to its "socialist" identity— is the "nationalist" card that Samaras, the new leader elected after the resignation of Karamanlis, is in a good position to play, given his past conflict with the party establishment on nationalist issues. Particularly so, as PASOK is even more obedient to the transnational elite than New Democracy on "national" issues (Cyprus and Greek-Turkish relations, Macedonia, etc.). This, of course, is by no means surprising, given that Papandreou is well known as one of the most docile instruments of the transnational elite in the Greek political elite and Pangalos, his vice president, is a brazen adventurist who has shown in the past that he has no qualms to do any despicable act that his transnational bosses would ask him to do —as the Ocalan case[2] has clearly shown, when he played a leading role in trapping the Kurdish leader on behalf of the US and Turkish secret services and then effectively handed him over to his Turkish tormentors— just in order to satisfy his personal political ambitions.

As regards the parties of the Left, the Communist Party, although it is the only parliamentary party which has adopted a clear line against the participation of Greece in the institutions of the transnational elite in general and the EU in particular, yet, it has lost so far the unique opportunity that was created by the present deep crisis to raise the topical demand for an immediate break with the EU, beginning with an exit from the Eurozone. And this, despite the fact that today it is more than ever generally accepted that it was the integration of the country's economy into the internationalised market economy in general, and the EU in particular, which has led to the present disintegration of the country's production structure[3] and, consequently, to the current deterioration of the chronic economic crisis.

As far as the parties of the reformist Left is concerned, SYN, which belongs to the "European Left" (a reformist coalition of European parties which are fully integrated within the EU institutions), is only critical of the Maastricht Treaty and its Stability Pact, while it adopts Greece's integration into the EU and the EMU. However, at this moment of crisis, it seems that the Left wing of SYN is in a process of rethinking its EU orientation and tending towards some sort of coalition with some "radical left" components of

SYRIZA (an umbrella organisation of reformist Left groups to which SYN itself belongs), but it is not yet clear at this moment of writing whether the new radical grouping will proceed beyond the usual reformist Left policy of just criticising the Stability Pact of the Maastricht Treaty, but not the EU as a whole, despite the fact that under conditions of neoliberal globalisation, i.e. of open and liberated markets, the EU itself is unviable unless it adopts the fiscal criteria of this Treaty. The same contradiction characterises some parts of the Left to the left of SYRIZA (mostly Trotskyites) which, also, do not raise the issue of a unilateral exit from the EU and set instead utopian demands for a pan-European abolition of the Stability Pact —something that with the present composition of the EU— is unthinkable to ever be agreed on by most of its members, apart perhaps from a few members in the European South (what markets call "the PIGS" [!] i.e. Portugal, Italy/Ireland, Greece and Spain). Finally, the libertarian Left seems to be dominated by a so-called "anti-authoritarian" tendency (AK), which is very close to the Znet empire (the US self-declared "anarchist" movement of Chomsky, Albert, the late Zinn and others), well known for its reformist tendencies covered under "anarchist" rhetoric.[4]

Lastly, the Greens propose a "Green growth" kind of process, in the form of a "green" capitalism, which has already become a big "business" in the international scene and is promoted by the elites of every persuasion, clearly out of potential profit considerations rather than out of their concern about the imminent ecological threat. However, green capitalism, although useful in advanced capitalist countries like Germany where it might well give rise to extra production and employment in producing renewable energy apparatus (wind turbines, solar panels, etc.) or green products (e.g., green cars), in countries in the periphery of the Eurozone like Greece —which do not have the required production structure and technology— it would simply increase further the level of imports and foreign debt, with some marginally positive results for consumers and the environment! Needless to add that the participation of several Green parties in European governments had hardly helped in restricting the impact of the continually deteriorating ecological crisis and that the only thing for which "radical" crooks of the European Greens like Daniel Cohn-Bendit and Joschka Fischer are remembered for is their direct or indirect support to the criminal wars of the transnational elite for the imposition of the New World Order![5]

Given the above positions of political parties, it does not come as a surprise that, according to the latest Euro-barometer, 85% of Greek citizens do not trust political parties, while 67% do not trust the Parliament itself! Although, there was never any doubt that the client system in Greece (complemented by compulsory voting) would eventually "work" in the last election as well —as it actually did— yet, abstention from what "passes as politics" seemed to be the only consistent choice with the Euro barometer's conclusions. And indeed, as we shall see next, abstention did play a prominent role in the Greek election results.

In fact, the election results demonstrated clearly the bankruptcy of the political system. Thus, the two parties, which have been running Greece for the past 35 years (i.e. the centre-left PASOK and the centre-right New Democracy Party) managed to attract only 30% and 23%, respectively, of registered voters. The reason is, of course, that the long-term growth of electoral absenteeism (expressed by abstention, and the casting of blank or invalid votes which is usually deliberate in Greece), was confirmed once more, as it has been amply shown by the fact that the rate of absenteeism in the above sense has grown by 14% between the 2004 and 2007 elections, and by an additional 11% between the elections in 2007 and 2009. As a result, this rate is now close to 32%, compared to about 20% for the entire period from mid 1970's until the beginning of the last decade! However, if in a clearly client political system such as the Greek one, the two establishment parties can just manage to attract only half of the registered voters, then, the political system is certainly in serious crisis!

Yet, the political crisis does not only concern the establishment parties, but also the traditional Left, parliamentary and extra-parliamentary, which has just managed to hit 13% of the votes, presenting even a small decrease of its power compared with the last parliamentary elections. This, at the very moment when the internationalised market economy in general was confronted with an unprecedented crisis like the present one, and the Greek economy in particular was facing an even worse crisis due to its distorted "development"![6] Of course, these results were not unlike similar trends in Europe as a whole. Thus, it is not only the social democratic parties which have been collapsing everywhere following their adoption of social-liberalism. The Green parties have passed through a similar crisis, after becoming everywhere a leading support of the system, mainly appealing to the middle classes that have basically solved their survival problems —not surprisingly, the Greek Greens collected their highest number of votes in the luxury "northern suburbs" of Athens. Besides, the Green parties have become for a long time the "Left boot of the system",[7] as it is shown by their despicable stand of either directly supporting the wars of the transnational elite, or keeping "equal distances" on crucial issues like Palestine, in return, of course, for the role of the "legitimate" opposition to the system that the former anti-systemic Green movement is reduced to play today, the lavish subsidies to their party funds from the EU funds and the scandalous salaries of the members of European Parliament![8]

Economic bankruptcy and "green" development

However, as I recently tried to show in this Journal, [9] the present international crisis is not only economic (namely, a crisis which is a symptom of the chronic crisis of the system of capitalist market economy), but also, political, ecological and social. In other words, it is a systemic multi-dimensional crisis. In Greece, the chronic economic crisis, which is expressed in the post-war period by the dismantling of the production structure that was brought to completion with the opening of its markets to the world market —a process that was accelerated by its integration into the EU at the beginning of the 1980s— has been accompanied by a corresponding chronic crisis of the political system. This crisis deteriorated with the outbreak of the current financial crisis and it became all too obvious by the social explosion of December 2008, [10] followed a few months later by the effective resignation of the New Democracy government at the end of the Summer 2009 and the ensuing general election at the beginning of October.

The effective dismantling of the productive structure inevitably led to the continuous growth of the external debt as well as of the public debt —the latter reaching an explosive point in the eve of the elections. No wonder that the Governor of the Bank of Greece, representing the economic elite, waited for the victory of PASOK, the preferred party by the economic elite, to be announced, before revealing that the budget deficit exceeded 10% of the GDP (a figure to be revised upwards later to 12.5%) and describing the extent of the crisis in the public finances —something that was well known to the political and economic elites before the elections. A crisis, which has resulted in Greece being formally placed initially under the European Commission's "surveillance", with the aim to force the political elite to follow strict "adjustment programs" in order to drastically reduce the budget deficit and that of the balance of payments. Of course, this does not imply anymore that, failing this, the fleets of foreign lenders will besiege Greek ports to supervise compliance with the conditions imposed —as it did actually happen in the last major bankruptcy of the Greek state at the beginning of 20th century! Nowadays, the economic and political-military mechanisms that can ensure compliance with these conditions (which are based on social-liberal reforms aiming at squeezing the social insurance and public sectors, "flexible" work, etc.) are already "inside the walls". It was not accidental that one of the first acts of the new social-liberal government was to rename the Ministry of the National Economy to add "competitiveness" in its title. The signal was that any direct or indirect economic activity (namely, almost every social function) must now be judged by the criteria of the market economy: from the mode of operation of the National Health Service and of public transport to that of the University. The obvious aim of the new social-liberal government, whose model is the American and British social-liberals (Obama and Blair/Brown, respectively) is for everything to become "business", functioning according to market criteria. And of course, those who resist this process and take to the streets will have to face the "Ministry for Citizen's Protection" (sic!), i.e. the renamed —according to the US elites' standards of political correctness and the Orwellian criteria— former Ministry of Public Order, with all its noble armour (chemicals, plastic bullets —if not real ones— etc.!).

Furthermore, economic developments in late November made even more urgent for the local elites the need to implement drastic economic "reforms". Thus, a speculative attack against sovereign bonds (namely, bonds issued by the Greek state to borrow from commercial banks which buy them) led the economy on the brink of bankruptcy and to a new intervention of the European elites to "save" it, imposing of course their own conditions. Naturally, these developments did not —nor could they— lead, anyway, to the formal bankruptcy of the Greek state. It would obviously be unthinkable for a member of the EMU to declare bankruptcy, not only on account of the possible serious damage to the Eurozone's "prestige", but also because it would potentially put at risk the stability of Euro itself. Especially, when other countries of the periphery/semi-periphery in the EU face similar problems —mainly, the PIGS. However, the price to be paid, particularly by the lower income strata (workers, employees, under-employed, unemployed and pensioners) in the coming years, will be very heavy indeed (see last section).

But, how did Greece come to the brink of bankruptcy? Initially, it should be noted that this has been a cumulative process rather than a sudden development. In fact, the economic and political elites led the economy to the brink of bankruptcy, with their acts and omissions, throughout the post-war period. In other words, today's effective (though not formal) bankruptcy is clearly a systemic problem, which is not only related to the current global crisis and the policies of the New Democracy party, as the professional politicians of PASOK claim, "forgetting" the crucial role of their own party in the creation and enhancement of the cumulative process that led Greece to its present situation!

In fact, both the external debt and the public debt began exploding immediately after joining the EEC in the 1980s, which coincided with the rise of PASOK to power [11]. Thus, the external debt was mainly created because of the fact that the economic and political elites left the entire development process virtually to the market forces, creating the paradox of a "consumer society without a production basis". The inevitable result was that Greece got used to consume much more than what it produced and, correspondingly, exported goods and services of a value that represented a small fraction of the value of those imported. At the same time, the public debt also exploded, because PASOK, under its founder (the father of the present PM) attempted in the 1980s, as soon as they took over, to combine the consumer society being created with a rudimentary welfare state. But the latter was supposed to be created not through a redistribution of income, which as a socialist party espoused (i.e., by taxing heavily the tax evasive privileged social strata to which many of its supporters belonged), but through heavy borrowing. This, through the growing payments for debt servicing, led to a vicious circle of debt accumulation. As a result, the public debt as a percentage of GDP increased more than five times within just six years, from about 8% of GDP in 1979 to over 42% in 1985 and, correspondingly, the total external debt (public and private) quadrupled within the same period from 13% of GDP to 50% [12]. Inevitably, government spending rose from an average 28.8% of GDP in the 1970s, to 41.1% in the 1980s[13], and over one third of this increase in spending was due to the huge increase in service payments on government debt, which more than tripled as a percentage of GDP.[14] Since the 1980s both the public debt and the external debt have increased three times, and, according to the Deutsche Bank, the public debt is today about 135% of GDP while the external debt has reached the 150% mark![15] Thus, even according to the conservative calculations of the new Budget, a quarter of the total public revenue will be used for interest payments. That is, over 5% of GDP (which is more than double the rate of the 1980s) will be spent on interest, so that the Greek elites can continue to borrow further!

This does not, of course, mean that these loans benefited production, since they were merely used for consumption purposes, as is evidenced by the fact that during the same period the effective dismantling of the manufacturing and agricultural sectors was also completed, as it is indicated by the growing trade deficit, as a result of our accession to the EEC and later the entry to the EMU, which made even less competitive the Greek exports. For example, it is estimated that from the beginning of the decade to date the Euro has become dearer by 20%. [16] Nor did these loans benefit the public, and especially the lower income strata that, mainly, bear the burden of these debts, given that indirect taxes hurt disproportionately these social strata, despite the fact that they are the only ones who dutifully pay their taxes.

Thus, public spending on education and health, as a proportion of GDP, in 1988, after seven years of "socialist" government, was only half of that in the European countries of OECD.[17] Today, it is still 66% of that in the EU

—although in the meantime Greek public debt has quadrupled![18] Furthermore, even official data show a highly skewed income distribution, with the 20% of the poorest receiving today less than 7% of income, while 20% of the richest receive almost 42% and Greece showing a significantly higher degree of inequality than the EU average.[19] Furthermore, as I will show in the last section, the latest barbarous measures imposed on the Greek people by the EU and Greek elites are bound to further deteriorate a very unequal distribution.

In the midst of the worst deterioration in the chronic Greek economic crisis on record, PASOK, followed by the reformist Left (SYN) and the mainstream Greens propose the panacea of "green growth". However, assuming green growth is feasible in countries at the level of development of Greece, it would still be undesirable as a means of creating income and employment, let alone as a means to deal with the worsening ecological crisis, for the following reasons:

• First, because no "tidying up" of public spending (an old Thatcherite slogan implying savage public spending cuts) and "cracking down on tax evasion" (a permanent slogan of the Greek elite) would be adequate to finance such a growth. As the public assets still available for privatisation are rapidly running out, following the selling out of the nation's silverware by previous governments, it is obvious that the only way for funding such a policy is either further borrowing or foreign investment. However, the former would not only directly contravene the Maastricht stability criteria (which have already been dramatically violated by Greece), but it would also inevitably lead to a further downgrading of the country's ratings by the credit agencies —a development that would surely lead to more onerous borrowing terms in the future, further enhancing the vicious circle of debt. And the chances of the latter are even smaller now than they used to be, given the deep recession to which Greece has been condemned by the latest EMU measures,

• Second, because any attempt by the Greek ruling elite to minimise the effects of the crisis through some sort of "green' growth" —instead of the favoured austerity by the EU elite for member-countries heavily indebted like Greece— is impossible, unless it represents the consensus of the elites controlling EMU. Moreover, it is not accidental that the only countries that have attempted a similar policy to deal with the present crisis, US and UK, have their own currency. This means that only at EMU level could similar policies be implemented and not by member countries on their own, given the potential impact of such "Keynesian" policies on the stability of the common currency. It is also highly indicative that out of the two countries mentioned above which followed such policies, only the US has not experienced problems with the stability of its currency, simply because Chinese investors still have confidence in the dollar. Britain, on the other hand, saw the value of Sterling collapsing since the last year or so, as a result of the huge rise in its public debt. No wonder, its political elite is presently forced to adopt savage cuts in public investment, and

• Finally, because "green growth" mainly benefits the countries which can produce green products (cars, appliances, etc.) and equipment for the creation of renewable energy (wind turbines, solar panels, wave power, etc.), so as to benefit both directly (from additional production) and indirectly (from cheaper consumption, etc.). That is why the elites in countries like Germany (with the strong support of the Greens) fight for green growth, i.e. not only because they consider it as a good tool to overcome the ecological crisis, but also, because it is big "business". However, countries in the periphery of EMU, like Greece, which import almost everything, not only are they not going to expand income and employment by adopting a green growth process, but, also they will help to the further deterioration of the structural problems of the Greek economy and, in particular, of the balance of payments and the foreign debt. In other words, the only benefit for Greece from green growth would, mainly, be on the side of consumption (lower energy cost) and only indirectly on the side of production, (e.g. because of the creation of some jobs in the trade of green products, the installation and maintenance of wind turbines, solar panels, etc.).

Social crisis and the systemic problem of immigration

To this political and economic bankruptcy, one has to add the worsening social crisis, as manifested by the "old" problems of the expansion of drug abuse[20] and crime, as well as the new growing problem created by the massive influx of immigrants (another clearly systemic problem).

Thus, the new "socialist" government, not only, as we saw above, is already taking the worst economic measures against the lower social strata in living memory, but it also continues and expands further the state repression of the last government. This repression is not only manifested against the "usual suspects", that is, the young (mostly unemployed) people, who are baptized "hooligans" by the "energetic" Minister for the "protection" of civilians (who has received US training on policing methods!) and the current "wretched" of the system, the immigrants. As from its early days, the new government, walking on the steps of the previous one [21], began using brutal force against "unruly" workers and citizens who dared to protest against the atrocities of the police and the related racist pogroms.

Prosecutions against immigrants are not, of course, a new phenomenon. In the EU, only in 2008, there were 146,337 arrests of immigrants (that constitute 24.5% of total arrests!), representing an increase of 65% compared with 2006.[22] The mass arrests in Greece followed the announcement of draconian legislation in July last year, which included dramatically extending the amount of time undocumented migrants can be detained. And, despite widespread protests from Greeks and migrant groups over the prospect of "migrant concentration camps" being created, the conservative government has also floated the idea of detaining "illegals" in disused military facilities. [23] It is therefore clear that, as Simone Troller points out, "other EU member states are all too willing to look the other way as Greece performs their dirty work of keeping migrants out."[24] No wonder, therefore, that the UN High Commission for Refugees inspectors described as unacceptable the conditions of detention of immigrants, stressing, for example, that more than 850 people, among whom 200 were unaccompanied children, mostly from Afghanistan, were detained under appalling conditions in Pagani of Lesbos. Nor is it, of course, accidental that "Greece's notorious asylum process has the lowest acceptance rate in Europe. Of the 20,000 applicants last year, asylum was accorded to only 379".[25]

However, the question is what really changed since the beginning of the decade, when the elites in Europe and in Greece turned a blind eye to the massive —legal or illegal— influx of immigrants from the periphery (Asia, Africa, etc.) and semi-periphery (Eastern Europe)? In fact, what has, mainly, changed is the deterioration of the chronic economic crisis, which has led to the present explosion of unemployment in Western Europe —at an enormous political cost to the elites— that endangers the system itself. In Greece, in particular, the economic crisis had begun deteriorating earlier, when, following the 2004 Olympics, the country was left with an even bigger debt than before while the construction explosion, which was based on cheap immigrant labour, rapidly subsided.

A crucial role on the ups and downs of immigration is played by the opening and liberalisation of markets in the present era of neoliberal globalisation, which has led to a huge concentration of economic power, income and wealth to economic elites and the privileged social strata.

However, while the liberalisation of the markets for commodities, capital and labour ("flexible" labour relationships) was complete, that was not also the case as regards the opening of these markets. The opening of the labour market has always been controlled by the transnational elite, so that the inflow of cheap labour in the North could be regulated, in accordance with the needs of the economic elites and the economic conjuncture.

The economic and political advantages to the elites from immigration are obvious. Not only does cheap immigrant labour reduce the cost of production and directly improves productivity and competitiveness, but it also plays a role in depressing real wages of local labour, leading indirectly to a parallel expansion of competitiveness. From the political and cultural perspective, immigration is the modern form of the historically tried out policy of "divide and rule", through which the elites usually perpetuated their dominance. Thus, foreign workers are blamed by the yellow press and TV channels as the source of the present multidimensional crisis, with problems such as unemployment, the explosion of crime, the crisis of the welfare state (imposed by neoliberal globalisation through cutting up social spending for the sake of competitiveness) as well as cultural homogenisation (another by-product of globalisation) —all attributable to immigrants. In this way, the real culprits of the multidimensional crisis (the economic and political elites and the privileged social strata) [26] are exonerated from responsibility, while the lower social and economic strata are persuaded to see the social "enemy" in the usually even poorer immigrants! A growing culture of xenophobia[27] is cultivated directly or indirectly by the elites, which, in several European countries, becomes even nastier when it is combined with Islamophobia, like the one promoted by Geert Wilders in Holland, whose neo-fascist Freedom Party did tremendously well in the March local elections —a fact which positions him well for the general election, with his Party now being forecast to emerge as the first or second largest in parliament.[28] No wonder that Britain, which last year banned his entry into the country, this year changed its mind and allowed him to give a lecture in Parliament about the "terrorism" that Islamism represents!

Of course, all this does not mean that mass immigration is not a problem for workers. However, in reality, this is a systemic problem which is produced and reproduced by the very system of the capitalist market economy and its dynamics. Thus, the dynamics created by the opening and liberalisation of markets, in the context of the present economic globalisation, led to the de-industrialisation of the "North" and the corresponding creation of some economic bubbles of the "South" (China, India and the rest). The combined effect of the mass inflow of capital to the bubbles of the South —which have been transformed into the assembly lines of transnational corporations from the North— and of the reverse inflow of cheap commodities and labour to the North, not only led to the massive expansion of long term unemployment and poverty in the North and to the dismantling of local economic self-reliance in the South, but it also played a crucial role in the world financial crisis[29] which has now been transformed into a debt crisis. At the same time, political globalisation, namely the need for full integration of the whole of the world (and particularly the crucial energy-rich Middle East) into the internationalised market economy, led to the criminal wars of the transnational elite in Afghanistan, Iraq, etc., which have added huge "armies" of political refugees to the millions of economic refugees.

The move of PASOK from social-liberalism to social-fascism

The newly elected social-liberal government attempted, initially, through a massive communications campaign, decisively helped by the media (most of which are sympathetic to PASOK, whereas state TV and radio play a clear propaganda role in favour of the government and the Prime Minister personally), to create a favourable image of a revamped party, which was determined to break with the past and create a new prosperous Greece rid of old practices (massive tax evasion, corruption, etc.). In this framework, the government attempted first to create a false impression of redistributing income. False, because with one hand it was making some petty extra payments to lower income groups in the form of a lump sum allowance, while with the other it was increasing indirect taxes which primarily hit the same social strata! Particularly so, as it left the relatively low direct taxes on income (personal and corporate) untouched —a recipe that surely leads to further deterioration of an already highly unequal distribution of income.

At the same time, the government engaged in a massive media "transparency" campaign, of a kind very reminiscent of "mirrors for the cannibals"! Thus, Papandreou, assuming the role of a supreme ruler who wants to be "close to his people," was almost daily seen on TV visiting numerous state services to see for himself whether they serve well his "subjects" and issue corresponding "directives" to the civil servants involved, or, functioning as a kind of mini-US President, he was seen presiding over "open," clearly staged, Cabinet meetings, which were highlighted for hours live by state television, and where ministers were seen reading ready-made insubstantial speeches (enriched with diagrams, etc.). The show clearly aimed to create the image of transparency, when, of course, it is well known that real decisions are not even taken by the

Cabinet, but by the think tank around the PM and his close family!

At the same time, the Orwellian Ministry "for citizen's protection" unleashed a campaign of increasing repression, not only against the "usual suspects," i.e. the youth who rose up in December 2008 and the immigrants, but also against "unruly" workers who dared to challenge it, with the right to strike being the first to suffer from the new "socialist" government. Thus, the strike of the dockers against the privatisation of the biggest port in the country, the port of Piraeus, was effectively suppressed by the executive part of the elite, the judiciary, which declared the strike as "illegal" because it openly aimed at the privatisation of the port —an aim that the political elite had already taken care to declare "political" and, therefore, illegal, in a process where the political and judicial power, in perfect harmony, confirm the Greek folk wisdom "John offers a drink and John drinks"! Similarly, the strike by one of the poorest sectors of society, the municipal dustmen who work under temporary contracts, was also declared "illegal" by the courts, with the consent, of course, of the "socialist" government, which obviously had no qualms about strangling the right of even the poorest workers in Greece to strike!

Then, it was the turn of the youth which was determined to commemorate the killing of a fifteen years old student by the police in December 2008. A massive police operation was launched to deal with it, whereas the Athens area where the killing took place, had effectively been transformed, since the PASOK taking over, into a police-controlled ghetto, leading to frequent clashes between residents and the police. Mass arrests and brute force were used to terrorise the protesting youth with police on motorbikes chasing rioters (leading to the serious injury of a woman demonstrator who was hit by a police motorcycle) and firing mass volleys of teargas and chemicals (allegedly bought from Zionist Israel, which of course has a long experience in violently suppressing popular resistance!) to disperse the youths in running street battles in the centre of the capital.[30] Clearly, the message was that no mass protest, of the scale of December 2008, will be tolerated in the dark future that was already dawning in Greece.

However, the descent of the Greek social-liberal party towards semi-totalitarianism is far from a local phenomenon. It well reflects a general trend which has transformed the European ex-social democratic parties and presently social liberal ones into social-fascist parties. But, social-fascism today takes a very different form from the old image used by the Comintern to describe the social democratic parties in the 1930s. Social-fascism then was supposed to be a variant of fascism, in the sense that it stood in the way of the final transition to communism. Today, social-fascism takes the form of a mix of spurious social democracy and semi-totalitarian "democracy," [31] as the inevitable outcome of the adoption by the ex-social democratic parties of the necessary social-liberal policies to make them conform with the present neoliberal globalisation of open and liberated markets. This outcome was inevitable, because it was only through massive, preventive as well as repressive, systemic violence that the present reversal of the social democratic achievements, which were realised during the statist period (1945-mid of 1970s), could be consolidated. Thus, the disintegration of the welfare state, through the effective dismantlement of fundamental social services (free education, national health systems, comprehensive social security arrangements, etc.), with the ultimate aim to fully privatise them; the massive unemployment and underemployment following the massive cuts in public spending; the introduction of "flexible" labour relations; and more importantly, the enormous concentration of economic power in the hands of the privileged social strata that has led to the present monstrous levels of inequality in the distribution of income and wealth —all these could not have been achieved without being effectively "shielded" from popular counter-violence, namely, the defence of the weaker social strata against the mass systemic (economic as well as physical) violence.

No wonder, therefore, that cameras have been installed everywhere in major cities like London, supposedly to protect citizens from crime; citizens are humiliated when travelling even to the extent of being forced to have an electronic striptease before being allowed to travel; demonstrators are violently suppressed when they dare to blame the transnational elite for the present multidimensional crisis (e.g. in London during the G20 meeting, then in Copenhagen during the climate conference, etc.); the right to strike is effectively suppressed through the banning of wildcat or sympathetic strikes, inevitably leading to the consolidation of the power of trade union bureaucrats (who are usually controlled by the elites); telephone and internet communication is closely monitored by "Big Brother" and so on.

The case of the transformation of the British Labour Party from a social-liberal to a purely social-fascist party in the above sense is clear and it is obviously the model used by PASOK in Greece. The British social-liberals, on the pretext of war against "terrorism" (which they have created in the first place by invading countries like Afghanistan and Iraq), have led to a police state system of mass surveillance (cameras, internet, etc.) and repression of all forms of popular counter violence. [32] No wonder that even an ex-head of the anti-terrorism service now claims that Britain under Labour social-liberals "is sliding towards a police state!".[33]

Social-fascism, like the original Fascism, requires the parallel development of a sophisticated propaganda system that will ensure a significant degree of popular support. Furthermore, it needs a system that will foster fear and suspicion in citizens, even for their neighbours. This irrational fear and insecurity —which is also cultivated by the whole sub-culture of Hollywood and television serials— is already bearing fruit in Greece where, according to a recent poll, nearly 60% of people stated that they feel being "in danger". [34] Indeed, today's social-fascist regimes have a very powerful tool in their hands, which the fascist regimes could not even dream of: television. Television plays the role of "manufacturing consent", not only through panel discussions, etc. in which the guests are carefully chosen to express the systemic views, but even more so through the way they present news. This way, a virtual reality is created which essentially has no relation to the actual reality and, given that most people nowadays learn about reality sitting in their sofas and few could be characterised in any meaningful sense as active citizens, effectively two worlds have been created: the world as seen and created in TV and the actual world. This blatant contradiction is being used to the full by the new PASOK government in Greece and the modern communication techniques obviously helps it on this task to distort reality, as seen by the average citizen.

It is, therefore, obvious that PASOK (which was selected by the local and foreign elites in preference to the New Democracy party, so that the deepening economic crisis could be dealt with in a way that would minimise the effect on the elites themselves and the privileged social groups) had to complement such measures with the corresponding social-fascist measures of mass surveillance and repression, to tackle the inevitable popular counter violence. Thus, the strangulation of strikes through legalistic means was followed by the implementation of a "zero tolerance" policy —a clearly totalitarian policy which, when applied by the military Junta in 1967-74 was considered "undemocratic," but now, when applied by the pseudo-democratic regimes all over the world (following the US semi-totalitarian example), it has been re-baptized as democratic! The pattern is well known: the political and economic elites, which control the economic and political process, initially institutionalize the arrangements that produce and reproduce the concentration of power in their hands, and then they go on to institutionalise as unlawful any substantial resistance to these measures and repress it accordingly.

The transformation of Greece into a EU protectorate

At the beginning of February, the European Commission announced plans which The Guardian characterised, with the usual British kind of understatement, as "the most intrusive scrutiny of an EU member state's fiscal and economic policies and book-keeping ever attempted", while the Commissioner himself stated, "this is the first time we have established such an intense and quasi-permanent system of monitoring," —a system that involved a stiff regime of quarterly reports from the Greek government on progress towards fiscal probity and the EC right to order extra action if needed.[35] This was followed a month later by the announcement (made by the Papandreou government on behalf of the EC —although they kept the pretence that they have designed themselves the measures!) of swingeing spending cuts and huge tax rises hitting the lower social groups. These measures involved, in a nutshell, shaving off a month's salary from the already low (by Eurozone standards) incomes of people employed in the public sector (who are estimated to be about one million, i.e. 20% of the total labour force), squeezing of public spending, rises in indirect taxes, including VAT, freezing of pensions and worsening of social security conditions with respect to pensionable age, etc.

At the same time, a huge media campaign was launched by the political elite to persuade the victims (employees, pensioners, unemployed, etc.) and lower income strata in general to bear once more the burden of the crisis. Inevitably, a huge "river of anger" has been pouring since then in the streets of Athens and other major cities, in repeated general strikes, in face of the mockery of local elites who are blatantly trying to transfer the impact of the measures imposed by the transnational elite —through the EU— to the lower social strata. Particularly so, as it is more than obvious that the measures announced will neither catch the enormous tax evasion, nor shall they force repatriation to the country of the billions of euros, already escaped abroad in the last couple of months since the crisis was announced, to be added to at least 60 billion euros which had already fled the country![36] However, had these funds and the local wealth been subjected to a significant proportionate extra property tax (something which is of course inconceivable for the elites), the famous problem of debt could have been solved in a flash, without having to beg for help and for new loans from the foreign elites, which (with profit in mind of course!) have been imposing instead onerous conditions that the future generations will have to pay for many years to come. This, despite the fact that it was the same elites and privileged social strata that created —and primarily benefited from— the debt, as shown, for instance, by the significant deterioration in the degree of inequality in the distribution of income in the last 30 years or so and the fact that, according to the official statistical data, almost 20% of Greek population are at the margin of poverty struggling to survive. It is also worth noting that Greece is the joint record holder with another PIGS member (Spain) as regards the size of poverty in the Eurozone.

But, let us examine briefly the mythology used by the media propaganda of the elites to justify the unprecedented structural measures against the lower social groups, as well as the real causes of the current crisis.

— First Myth: The primary responsibility for the crisis lies with the speculators who caused a tsunami of negative speculation against the Greek government bonds, or (if we accept the plot theories), against the euro as a whole, with a view to profit. In reality, however, to blame the speculators for speculating is like blaming the military for killing in war! Obviously, this is their job in the system of market economy: to find the weakest links in the system and engage in speculation to maximise their profits. In other words, all that speculators can do is to make a bad situation worse, but not to create it in the first place, and as we saw above, the Greek debt problem had begun exploding since the 1980s. So, all that speculators can do is to bring down the prices of sovereign bonds (and correspondingly push their yields up) affecting the rates at which the country concerned borrows in the world markets and possibly the "ratings" of the international agencies, leading to a vicious circle which may make refinancing the existing debt more difficult. Papandreou's effective propaganda machine presented the speculators as the main culprit for the crisis, simply in order to be able afterwards to present his "marathon" of trips to the main capitals of the transnational elite (Germany, USA, France, etc.) —at the expense of course of the Greek taxpayer who has to pay for the luxury trips of Papandreou and various ministers and advisers, even members of his family!— as well as the painless (for the elites) promises that they will help in the control of speculation, as a kind of personal "success" and at the same time divert the attention of the angry Greek people from the measures he has been imposing on them.

— Second Myth: Greece is on the verge of bankruptcy and Greeks have to make sacrifices to save their country, as such an eventuality would lead to the loss of sovereignty. In reality, however, although Greece is actually on the verge of bankruptcy, as I showed above, it is not in interest of the EU elites to allow such a development, either politically or economically, and therefore they will certainly provide financial help of some form to prevent such an outcome, of course on their own (strict —and beneficial to them) terms. Yet, this is an "exogenous" factor, which does not in any way question the fact that Greece is really the weak link, despite the attempted alchemy of figures by some (reformist Left) analysts, who went a step further and even attempted to show that Greece is not near bankruptcy at all, as supposedly is shown by the fact that an attempt by the state in the midst of the crisis to sell state bonds of about €5bn was oversubscribed or, alternatively, because similar levels of budget deficit and public debt characterise other members of the Eurozone as well. What however, they "forget" to mention is that although neither the public debt nor the budget deficit, in relation to GDP, are by themselves, the highest in the Eurozone, neither of the other member countries does it pose a similar combination of high rates (113% and 12.7% respectively).[37] Furthermore, no other Eurozone country has to repay or refinance, in just five years, half its total €300 b debt (mainly to German and French bankers) —€31b of which has to be repaid this year alone— and to spend more than half of the total government revenue in servicing the debt![38] Furthermore, any sovereign nation in the Eurozone could easily make similar loans to the recently oversubscribed one, particularly when it would have to pay, like Greece, an interest rate which was seven times as much as that of any commercial bank in the EU, while at the same time lenders do not face any real risk of losing their money, as they are fully aware that a member country of the Eurozone is never going to proceed to a compulsory expropriation of the debt, and that, one way or another, it will be finally forced to repay it in full! Finally, as regards the potential loss of sovereignty in case Greece becomes bankrupt, in fact, as we shall see, below, exactly the opposite is true: it is now that Greece has lost even the last vestiges of any kind of sovereignty!

— Third Myth: The EU itself has to be blamed for the crisis as it has no mechanism to prevent surpluses/deficits. Thus, the EU is blamed for not showing the necessary "solidarity" to a member state, by creating, for example, an economic union in addition to the monetary one. Moreover, as reformist economists emphasize [39] —taking of course for granted the entire institutional framework of open and liberalised markets and the EMU— the main culprit is the European Central Bank and the German elite which, thanks to the policy of "hard euro" it followed (which includes the suppression of labour costs), it improved significantly German competitiveness and consequently improved the German balance of payments, creating a significant surplus to it. Conversely, the faster increase in labour costs in countries like Greece has led to the decline of its competitiveness and it consequently worsened its balance of payments, further worsening its deficit —something that ultimately led to an increase in the public debt to finance the bubble of "growth" Greece enjoyed since its adoption of euro. And indeed, it is true that Germany, starting with a deficit of 1% of GDP in the Balance of Payments on Current Account in 2000, achieved a huge surplus amounting to 5% of its GDP today, while in the same period huge deficits were conversely created in the European South (Greece tripled the deficit in absolute numbers, Spain increased it as much as six times, etc.) and it is also true that, in the same period, labour cost in the European South has risen faster than that in the North. But, what such analyses "forget" is that, historically, wages were and still are, almost half in the South compared to those in the North (the minimum monthly wage in Greece, Spain and Portugal in 2006 was less than half of that in the European North[40]) and had a real convergence been achieved —supposedly a main EU policy— even greater differences in competitiveness would have been created among these countries, which no transfer of funds from a new institution (like the US Fed, as some suggest) would have been capable to eliminate. Particularly so when such convergence within a capitalist market economy has not been achieved even within nation-states (Italy, Germany, UK, etc.) let alone an economic union of states like the EU!

So, the EU is blamed by reformist analysts for the wrong reasons, i.e. for its internal organisation and structure —something that is hardly surprising coming from analysts who are only interested in improving the EU rather than in finding out whether there are any systemic reasons which intrinsically lead to crises like the ones that have been created at the moment in Greece and the PIGS in general. But, in fact, as it could be shown by both theory and historical experience, in any economic union consisting of members characterised by a high degree of economic unevenness (as is the case with the EU), the establishment of open and liberalised markets for commodities and capital, would inevitably lead to a situation where those which primarily benefit from the free movement of commodities and capital would be the more advanced regions/countries (which have already developed high productivity levels and advanced technologies) at the expense of the rest. No wonder therefore, that Greek productivity in manufacturing, in the period 1980-84, was about 42% of that in Germany and that after almost 20 years of membership, it was even lower at 38% in 1995-99![41] It is not therefore surprising that, historically, none of the presently advanced capitalist countries —which are now keen to promote the freedom of trade, etc.— opened its own markets before it has already achieved a high level of competitiveness for its own exports, under protected markets.

A clear case of how an entire production sector has effectively been dismantled, as a result of the opening and liberalisation of markets under EU rules, is the Greek agricultural sector, which, for almost every Winter in the last few years, has been in turmoil, with farmers blockading the main Greek roads —the last time in January of this year.

Thus, while the agricultural sector until Greece's accession to the EEC, in 1981, had been employing 31% of the active population[42] (against an average of 6% in the metropolitan centres of the EEC), following the accession, a general stagnation of agricultural production was recorded, despite the much-advertised subsidies through the CAP (Community Agricultural Policy). In fact, the agricultural population suffered a dramatic decline between 1981 and 2006, with the proportion of farmers in the total working population dropping by more than half in this period (from 31% in 1981 to 13% in 2006). The same of course happened in metropolitan countries as well, but while in these countries we talk about an approximately 3% of the active population which had to find (and basically found) employment in the expanding modern service sector, in Greece we talk about an 18% of the population, which had to turn to a parasitic "services" sector [43] to find employment. Moreover, while the reduction of the rural population in metropolitan centres did not prevent their agricultural production to continue growing rapidly (because of its greater productivity), in Greece it has completely stagnated. Thus, while the average annual growth rate of agricultural production in metropolitan centres in the period 1990-2006 was about 0.9%, the corresponding Greek rate was negative (—0.9%)! [44] And this, while in the two decades prior to accession (1961-81) Greek agricultural production was increasing at an average annual rate of 2.7%![45] Similar conclusions can be drawn about the effective dismantlement of the manufacturing sector following Greek entry to EU and EMU.

However, the above findings should not lead us to utopian conclusions and wishful thinking on the need for "self-organization" of farmers and the "regeneration of local communities," that supposedly would create "the conditions for establishing models of direct democracy". Self-organization by itself, within the existing institutions of the internationalised market economy and representative "democracy," either would lead to stagnation and eventual failure, or to integration in the system (see e.g. the case of Mondragon in Spain), since there cannot exist viable "islands" of an alternative organisation of production and society in general within an economy, such as the Greek one, that is fully integrated into the globalised market economy, through the EU. For instance, at what prices will the self-organized farmers dispose of their products when, in today's open and liberalised markets, on the one hand, the prices of their output (i.e. of their products) are determined by the lower cost of production which, ultimately, means the cheaper labour cost, and on the other, the prices of their "inputs" (i.e. of fertilizers, machinery, technology, etc.) are controlled by the multinationals? How can the "self-organized" farmers compete without "protection" against the agricultural products produced by India, China or Egypt, with their starvation wages, or even those produced by other EU countries or the US, with their higher productivity?

Is there an alternative solution to EU colonisation?

The predatory measures imposed on Greece by the Directorate of the EU, expressing the Eurozone's political and economic elites, clearly give the impression of a complete colonisation of the country by the transnational elite. This is not just about the implementation of neoliberal prescriptions of the EU in Greece, as claimed by some in the Left. It is one thing to implement similar measures by formal consensus of the people (as in Britain, Holland, Sweden, etc.) and quite another to enforce compliance with such measures, as it happens now in Greece. Especially when these measures do not have any popular legitimacy, given that the ruling party was elected on a program that provided for measures entirely different from those imposed now on the Greek people. This, despite the fact that the leadership of the ruling party (just as that of the New Democracy) was fully aware of the crisis —which is basically chronic— and deliberately deceived the electorate with the help of the political and economic elites controlling the media, assuming (rightly) that only a "socialist" party could have a chance to impose such measures, because of its comprehensive control of trade unions. And of course, no one can take seriously opinion polls paid for by private companies or parties, claiming strong political support for these measures. When "Greek statistics" is considered a kind of a joke in the Eurozone (as it is obvious now that they were compiled according to the wishes of the particular fraction of the Greek political elite in power at the time of compiling), it is clearly a kind of a bad joke to refer to the supposedly impartial findings of opinion polls, especially on such a crucial issue for the elites who finance these polls as the popular approval of the barbarous measures being imposed at the moment. The very fact that some polls have been published lately, which not only overturn the conclusions of the above fake polls but also show an overwhelming rejection of these measures, is a clear indication of this.

The enforced measures are presented, in a massive brainwashing by the elites and their acolytes in the media, as unavoidable. This however is true only if we take for granted the present institutional framework of today's globalisation, namely, open and liberalised markets, which are the ultimate cause along with the consequential treaties of Maastricht, Lisbon and the Stability Pact. In this context, competitiveness plays indeed a crucial role with respect to an exporting economy that bases its development on the free movement of commodities and capital (like Germany or China!). At the same time, competitiveness itself is related to low production costs which, in turn, are a function of wages, productivity, price stability, and also employers' contributions/taxes. The euro, therefore, cannot be separated from the Stability Pact, as is imprudently proposed by the reformist Left, because it is only when the common currency is complemented by criteria like those prescribed by the Stability Pact that, in the given institutional framework, monetary stability and the competitiveness of developed economies in the Eurozone can be achieved. In other words, without the policies of squeezing wages, prices and the associated deficits, the EU could not indeed survive in any competition with USA, China, etc. Therefore, the Eurozone was formulated on the basis of the needs of economies such as Germany's, which have little to do with the needs of countries like Greece, or other countries in the "European South".

So, the slogan "abolish the Stability Pact" is misleading, because it means, in fact, transferring the issue to be resolved within the EMU countries, something that presupposes a dramatic change in the overall balance of power within it and therefore postpones the implementation of this proposal to the indefinite future (if ever!). In the meantime, the Greek people will have gone down on their knees through an imposed neoliberal state of poverty and unemployment —something which nowadays usually leads to conservatism and apathy, as, for instance, in Britain. Similarly, the slogan of "disobedience to the EU" becomes rhetoric when the ruling party controls the main trade unions, out of which usually the future professional politicians in the party are selected!

On the other hand, however, an alternative "package" of measures could be proposed, which, even within the existing system of market economy and representative "democracy," would provide for:

• an exit from the current financial crisis (albeit not from the chronic economic crisis, which is associated with long term radical changes in the production and consumption structure of the country) without the current attack against social conquests and a consequent massive unemployment and poverty for decades to come,

• a genuine social justice (no relation to the one invoked by the government) for transcending the crisis, by forcing those, who have mainly benefited over the years by the massive borrowing, either directly (through the huge fortunes they have amassed by tax evasion, profiteering, etc.) or indirectly (through the huge increase in the value of their properties, as a result of the growth bubble that public borrowing made possible). On the other hand, the kind of social justice invoked by the EMU elites and the PASOK government involves the Governors of the European Central Bank and the Bank of Greece, who demanded (and got it!) the severe cuts on wages and salaries — including the trifling salaries paid to the young in their first job (the so-called in Greece "generation of 700 Euros"), whereas at the same time they themselves pocket 345,252 and 362,500 Euros respectively![46], and

• the creation of the preconditions for economic self-reliance (not self-sufficiency) and overcoming unnecessary consumerism in the future.[47]

The fundamental precondition for a similar "package" of measures is the recovery of national sovereignty that has now disappeared completely, even formally. Of course, Greece was never a fully sovereign country, as the modern Greek state that was established at the beginning of the 19th century, following a revolution against the Ottoman rule (a rule which lasted for almost four centuries), was in fact an informal protectorate of the powers that helped the Greek liberation (Tsarist Russia, Britain, France) and, following the demise of the Tsarist regime and the decline of French influence, it came under the political and economic tutelage of Britain. This was until the decline of the British empire and the rise of the American "empire," following the second world war and the defeat of the Left in the civil war (with the decisive military and economic help to the Right given by the Americans), created a new US protectorate (in all but its name) in Greece.

The political and economic elites in post-war Greece were completely dependent on the American elites, which did not have any qualms even to give the green light for the imposition of a military dictatorship in 1967, when a strong popular movement from below in the mid-1960s questioned the very political institutions on which American domination (centred around the Palace) was based. The military junta had further integrated the Greek economy into the internationalised market economy, relying on foreign investments and the foreign markets to boost an economic development of a purely dependent type.[48] It was during the military dictatorship period (1967-74) that a consumerist society was created in Greece, which, however, was based on an economic growth bubble, as the degree of self-reliance of the Greek economy was effectively being undermined with the gradual opening of the markets, which had led to an ever increasing gap between what the country could produce and what it was consuming, as it was shown by the fact that the trade deficit as a proportion of GDP has almost doubled from 9% in the 1950s to 16% in the 1970s.[49] This gap was initially covered by the remittances of millions of Greeks who were forced in the 1960s to emigrate to Germany, Australia, etc. to avoid unemployment and poverty at home, the shipping remittances (the Greek economic elites have always excelled in the shipping industry) and finally tourism, which was the emerging "heavy industry" for countries in the periphery and semi-periphery in the 1970s and 1980s. However, the first two sources began drying up in the 1980s when the demand for immigrants in the host countries was drastically reduced and Greek ship-owners began transferring their ships under various flags of convenience, reducing drastically Greek personnel in the process.

At the same time, Greece's integration into the internationalised market economy was sped up as a result of Greece's entry into the EEC, which not only led to the complete opening of its markets and a further loss of economic sovereignty through the loss of its right to protect its own agricultural and manufacturing sectors (leading to the inevitable effective dismantling of both!) but also led, when it joined the Euro at the beginning of last decade, to the formal end of a Greek monetary policy, which was determined since then by the European Central Bank (i.e. the economic elites of the Eurozone). Furthermore the Stability Pact of the Maastricht and Lisbon Treaties imposed strict controls on fiscal policy (the total debt level should not be higher than 60% of the GDP and the state budget deficit should not exceed 3% of it). In fact, as it has now been revealed, the Greek elites achieved these entry criteria only through "creative accounting," although Greece was not alone on this as other countries among the PIGS did the same to secure their entry, and most probably the European economic elites looked the other way, in order to expand the Eurozone.

So, the present takeover by the EU elites of even the last remnants of economic policy-making within Greece represents the completion of a long process, which presently formalises the transformation of Greece into an EU protectorate. Therefore, the first step in any attempt to recover economic sovereignty, which is a fundamental precondition for any restructuring of the Greek economic structure in a way that would make possible the control of the economic process by the Greek people themselves rather than by the foreign economic and political elites in collaboration with the local ones, is the immediate exit from the Eurozone, as a first step in the exit from the EU itself. In fact, an exit of Greece from the Eurozone —usually as a temporary measure and of course with a different rationale and a very different packet to complement it— is proposed presently also by distinguished orthodox or reformist economists like Martin Feldstein of Harvard University,[50] Erik Jones of Johns Hopkins University at Bologna,[51] or Dirk Meyer of Hamburg University,[52] contrary to Greek economists of the Left (Marxists and non-Marxists alike) who, following the establishment's line, predict a Greek economic catastrophe in case we exit from the Eurozone, usually without any serious arguments to support this view —something that creates a reasonable suspicion for those of them who are also academics that they have also vested economic interests in taking such a stand, given the heavy involvement of many of them in various research and teaching programs financed by the EU!

The first step, therefore, to be taken is an immediate referendum on whether the Greek people approve the predatory measures imposed on it by the Greek political elite on behalf of the Eurozone elite. This is actually the only way to legitimise these measures given that PASOK had blatantly deceived the Greek people in being elected on a program which promised exactly the opposite measures of the ones it now tries to implement. The centre-right New Democracy party was in fact more frank than the "socialists" of PASOK, as they did not hide their determination to freezing salaries, wages, etc., at the very moment when Papandreou and his clan were shamelessly lying to the people that they will proceed with increases in wages and salaries, in full knowledge of the size of the crisis they were facing (as I had revealed in my fortnight column at the Athens daily Eleftherotypia at the time[53]) and with the full support of the media controlled by the elites, which wanted at all cost to have a "socialist" government elected with the aim to deceive the people into submission — as they have succeeded so far in doing! The very fact that millions of people all over Greece are now taking part in repeated general strikes against the government measures and thousands take part in almost daily demonstrations against them, the conflicts which have already been created between the trade union bureaucrats controlled by PASOK (who desperately try to keep the social dissent controlled until it fizzles out) and the rank and file (which demands tougher union action to prevent the implementation of measures) are clear indications that the present brainwashing by the mass media is failing —a fact that is also confirmed by several "true" polls in contrast to the suspicious polls I mentioned above.

If, therefore, the political elite is interested even in keeping up the appearance of "democracy," it should proceed directly to a referendum for the approval or rejection of the predatory measures, so that the alternative proposals be publicly discussed —provided of course that conditions of absolute equality of the rights of participants in the media discussions are fully guaranteed. On the other hand, if the government continues imposing such measures without any legitimisation, then, it will not be any more a kind of "democratic" government of the usual Western representative "democracy" kind; it will be a pure "parliamentary junta" and will be treated correspondingly by the Greek people.

But, assuming a democratic referendum does take place and the present so called "stability program" implemented by the local elites on behalf of their foreign collaborator elites is rejected, what next? The next step, as I proposed above, is the immediate exit from the Eurozone but then the issue is: how the new currency to replace the euro would not be devalued significantly in foreign exchange markets under heavy speculation, and Greek capital will not move en mass out of Greece —possibilities that, if materialised, will force the lower social strata to pay an even higher price than before and possibly terrorise them to return to the present situation, marking a full circle?

Immediate measures following the rejection of the present elites' measures

In fact, however, there are ways to avoid, or at least minimise any such harmful side-effects. I would therefore propose a complementary "package" of measures, which could be implemented following a Greek exit from the EMU and the consequent release of Greece from the Stability Pact stipulations. These are measures that could be taken immediately following the rejection of the present ones by a referendum, which can be taken within the existing system of the capitalist market economy, and could set the preconditions for a self-reliant development in the future that could lead to an inclusive democracy in the long term. Such measures are:

a) a sensible devaluation of the "new drachma," which would be introduced in place of the euro —something that would make tourism and exports (particularly of agricultural products which are now suffering from an expensive euro) cheaper, and, at the same time, would make imported commodities more expensive —a development that would give significant protection to the local agricultural and manufacturing production. Imported basic necessities could be subsidised (so that the lower social strata would not pay higher prices to cover their basic needs) and the subsidies could be financed by the revenues generated through a heavy additional tax on imported luxury commodities, while strict price controls could prevent any unnecessary rise of prices,

b) a renegotiation of debt (under the threat of an immediate stoppage of payments in case this is not accepted), aiming at a significant lengthening of the period of its repayment and a corresponding reduction of the present exorbitant amount,

c) a gradual repayment of the renegotiated debt, through extra revenues generated mainly from a new and highly progressive tax on wealth, on any kind of property with a total value exceeding, for instance, €1m. The calculation of the tax to be paid could be based on the results of a general census of property located in Greece, as well as of deposits in foreign banks, etc., with the state proceeding to confiscate any property of a corresponding value to the estimated tax in case property owners declare inability to pay within a reasonable short period of time,

d) a parallel introduction of strict controls on capital movements, so as to stop any movement of speculative or non-speculative capital abroad (only in recent months the outflow of capital has exceeded 10 billion euros[54]), and protect the new currency from speculation.

The combination of these measures would mean the generation of more jobs and incomes, as well as a decrease in the hugely unequal distribution of income, in place of poverty and the greater inequality to which Greeks are condemned by the European and the local elites. However, given that the European and local elites show no intention of allowing a referendum to take place, as they are very well aware of the fact that —despite the massive propaganda campaign to create a kind of Orwellian truth, where "war is peace," or, in this case, "unemployment and poverty is freedom"— the result would surely be humiliating for them, the question is: what are the prospects for the future? To my mind, there are two possible scenarios "scenaria": a) the Latin-Americanisation of Greece, and b) the setting of the preconditions for economic democracy, as part of an Inclusive Democracy.

The prospects for the future of Greece

a. The scenario of Latin-Americanisation of Greece

According to the first scenario, the elites will push forward, no matter what, the present (and worse to come!) measures, which will lead to the Latin-Americanisation of Greece, a kind of Mexico within NAFTA, both at the political and the economic levels. In fact, there are indications that this process had already begun and it is funny indeed that some "critics" of my proposal for an exit from the EMU already stressed that such a step would mean the "Argentinisation" of Greece!

Thus, at the political level, Papandreou already behaves accordingly, and when for instance recently in Germany, begging Merkel for support, he had no qualms to respond as follows when asked to take a stand on the very offensive proposal made by German newspapers that Greece should sell some of its islands or national treasures to pay off its debt: "There are more imaginative and effective ways of dealing with the deficit than selling off Greek islands," and then he went on to explain these ways in terms of German investors investing on the "green growth" of the islands! Clearly, this is a response that no self-respecting leader will make, apart perhaps from the Prime Minister of a Latin American banana republic. And then again, when a few days later he was begging Obama for support, he declared, full of admiration like the district governor of a poor region, his complete support for the US's "fight against any form of tyranny and oppression" —i.e. to the mass crimes of the empire in Afghanistan and Iraq and the planned new crime in Iran!

At the economic level, implementation of the present measures will mean the continuation of present policies, rubber-stamped by PASOK, which is determined (despite the theatrical grumbling of some MPs) to vote on any bill proposed by the Leader, even a bill declaring that "pigs could fly," as long as they are kept in power, with all the financial and social benefits this secures for them. On this they will have the help of the docile trade union leaders close to them, who are ready to declare as "illegal" any strike which creates problems to the elites, and, also, the decisive help of the mass media, particularly the TV channels, with the state-owned channels playing a leading role in distorting the truth in a Goebbelian way and in praising the "Leader," in a not too dissimilar way to the role of their counterparts in praising Ceausescu! And, of course, with the crucial help of the security forces in suppressing any kind of annoying dissent against the predatory measures.

Inevitably, poverty will grow as a result of the implementation of the "stability program," as the direct result of the severe cuts in civil servants' salaries and in public spending, which will be complemented by the indirect negative effects on income (through the multiplier) that, according to the Deutsche Bank predictions, would mean a decline in the GDP by 4% this year alone, whereas the total decline of GDP during the implementation of the program in the next three years would be in the range of −12% up to −20%. Consequently, unemployment will become massive, as the already dismantled private sector has almost a null capability to absorb extra labour, whereas the traditional labour-absorbing sector, i.e. the public sector, will also become completely ineffective to continue this function in the future, as a result of the new measures. The combination of poverty and unemployment with the uneven effects of the increases in indirect taxes on low incomes will create even bigger inequality, in a country which is already among the most unequal countries in the Eurozone. The inevitable result would be the creation of a number of oases for the rich (locals and foreigners) in the midst of huge deserts in monster cities like Athens, where street gangs will shoot each other in drug wars —exactly as it happens in similar cities all over Latin America at the moment! Of course this does not mean, as a Castoriadian put it recently, that "the economic problem in Greece is political and is due to the corrupt and useless politicians, as well as to the institutional framework which promotes them" [55] with not a single word uttered about the socio-economic system, globalisation, and the EMU/EU —presumably because it is just the imaginary significations of the Greek people which have to be blamed for the present crisis! Similarly, the exit from the crisis cannot of course be achieved through "disobedience," as the supposedly "anarchist" Howard Zinn used to declare. Disobedience by itself could only lead to some improvements of the system or, at best, to easily suppressed insurrections but it would never lead, not it has ever led, to systemic changes. This brings us to the second possible scenario.

b. The scenario of setting the preconditions for an economic democracy as part of an Inclusive Democracy

According to this scenario, once the present measures are rejected through a referendum, and the immediate measures proposed above are implemented through the exit from the EMU and the Eurozone, a mass movement of self-organisation from below could develop and set the preconditions for self-reliance and economic democracy. Citizens could self-organise in every village, or neighbourhood, and begin building new institutions —outside the internationalised market economy— and increasingly rely on them to meet their needs.[56] It is only through the general assemblies of the citizens in such institutions, that the real public interest could be expressed, in contrast to the existing institutions, within which only the special interests of political and economic elites, and the social groups dependent on them, could really be expressed —an arrangement which has led to the current deep multi-dimensional and ever-worsening crisis.

Such a movement could proceed to the creation of:

a) new political institutions where all the important decisions are taken by the assemblies of the demos, i.e. the citizens' body assemblies in a highly decentralised society (decentralisation needs to be only administrative in the first instance) , which could send recallable delegates (not "representatives"), with specific mandates, to regional and confederal assemblies for implementing the principles and values decided at the local level in relation to regional and confederal problems (Political Democracy),

b) new economic institutions based on the collective ownership and control of the means of production and distribution, which will be leased free to the "demotic" enterprises (i.e. the enterprises which will be under the overall control of the demotic assemblies and will be self-governed through the assemblies of the employees in each enterprise). Such assemblies could implement the decisions included in a confederal plan for meeting the basic needs of each citizen, according to the principle "from each according to ability to each according to need". Freedom of choice as regards the satisfiers for basic needs (the means to satisfy the basic needs) as well as the non-basic needs themselves and their satisfiers could be secured through an artificial "market" (based on vouchers or on a demotic credit card system) that will replace the present market system (Economic Democracy),
c) new institutions for running each place of work or education based on

self-management and the abolition of any differentiation of people according to gender, race, nationality or cultural and sexual identity (Democracy in the social realm) and, last, but not least,

d) of a society which will be reintegrated with nature, through the replacement of the present growth economy based on an eco-catastrophic consumerism by an economy geared to meet the real needs of the people in ways that do not put at risk the quality of life, if not life itself, as at present (Ecological Democracy).

The combination of these four essential components of democracy (political democracy, economic democracy, democracy in the social realm and ecological democracy) constitute what we call an Inclusive Democracy.

In conclusion, it is imperative that the anti-systemic Left, in Greece and in Southern Europe as a whole (the so-called PIGS!), directly challenges the present European integration in terms of markets and capital and establishes instead a new confederation of European Inclusive Democracies, as a model for the integration of European peoples as a whole, within a pan-European confederation of Inclusive Democracies, which consolidates the equal distribution of political and economic power among European peoples, and among all citizens within each part of the confederation.

[1] See Takis Fotopoulos, "A systemic crisis in Greece," The International Journal of Inclusive Democracy, Vol. 5, No. 2 (Spring 2009). http://www.inclusivedemocracy.org/journal/vol5/vol5_no2_takis_systemic_c risis_greece.htm

[2] See T. Fotopoulos, "The global 'war' of the transnational elite," Democracy & Nature, Vol. 8, No. 2 (July 2002). http://www.democracynature.org/vol8/takis_globalwar.htm

[3] See Takis Fotopoulos, Globalisation, the Left and Inclusive Democracy (in Greek) (Athens, 2002), Ch. 9, "The consequences of the internationalisation of the Greek economy"; see, also, T. Fotopoulos,

"Economic restructuring and the debt problem", International Review of Applied Economics, Vol. 6, No. 1 (1992).
http://www.inclusivedemocracy.org/fotopoulos/english/brvarious/restruct_irae_92.htm

[4] See, T. Fotopoulos, The Pink Revolution in Iran and the "Left" (IJID, 2009) Ch. 5. http://www.inclusivedemocracy.org/journal/

[5] See Takis Fotopoulos, "The end of the Green movement as a liberation force?" in "The First War of the Internationalised Market Economy," Democracy & Nature, Vol. 5, No. 2 (July 1999).
http://www.inclusivedemocracy.org/dn/vol5/fotopoulos_balkans_2.htm

[6] See Takis Fotopoulos, Dependent Development: the case of Greece (in Greek) (Athens, 1985 & 1987).

[7] See my article "Iran: The campaign for regime change in its last phase" (in this Issue).
http://www.inclusivedemocracy.org/journal/vol5/vol5_no4_takis_iran_last_phase.htm

[8] Mats Persson , "The real expenses scandal is in Brussels," The Guardian (27/5/2009).
http://www.guardian.co.uk/commentisfree/2009/may/27/expenses-meps-european-parliament

[9] T. Fotopoulos, "The myths about the economic crisis, the reformist Left and economic democracy," The International Journal of Inclusive Democracy, Vol. 4, No. 4 (October 2008).
http://www.inclusivedemocracy.org/journal/vol4/vol4_no4_takis_economic_crisis.htm

[10] T. Fotopoulos, "A systemic crisis in Greece," The International Journal of Inclusive Democracy, Vol. 5, No. 2 (Spring 2009).
http://www.inclusivedemocracy.org/journal/vol5/vol5_no2_takis_systemic_crisis_greece.htm

[11] T. Fotopoulos, "Economic restructuring and the debt problem," op. cit.

[12] ibid., Table 1

[13] ibid., Table 4

[14] ibid.

[15] Wolfgang Münchau, "Greece can expect no gifts from Brussels," The Financial Times (30/11/2009).

[16] The Financial Times (25/11/2009)

[17] OECD, Economic Surveys: Greece (1990)

[18] World Bank, World Development Indicators 2008, Tables 2.10 & 2.15

[19] As it is shown by a comparison of the Gini coefficients, ibid., Table 2.8

[20] T. Fotopoulos, Drugs: beyond the demonology of penalisation and the "progressive" mythology of liberalization (in Greek) (Athens, 1999).

[21] Helena Smith, The Guardian (3/12/2007).

[22] Barnaby Phillips reporting in Al Jazeera (28/8/2009).

[23] Helena Smith, The Observer (27/9/2009).

[24] See e.g., Simone Troller, The Observer (25/1/2009).

[25] See the Athens daily Eleftherotypia (29/8/2009).

[26] See T Fotopoulos, The Global Crisis, Greece and the Antisystemic Movement (in Greek) (Koukkida, 2009), Part on

[27] See the Greek ID network brochure on "Racism as the inevitable symptom of hierarchical structures and relations" (in Greek) (July 2009). http://www.inclusivedemocracy.org/brochures/2009.7__ratsismos_antiratsi stiko_festival.htm

[28] Peter Mair, "Huge influx of immigrants has changed Dutch society forever," The Independent (5/3/2010).

[29] T. Fotopoulos, "The myths about the economic crisis, the reformist Left and economic democracy," op. cit.

[30] See A. Carassava, "Greece running out of patience with anarchy," The Independent (11/12/2007) ; AP, "Riots grip Athens on anniversary of death," The Guardian (7/12/2009).

[31] See T. Fotopoulos, The Global Crisis, Greece and the Antisystemic Movement (in Greek) (Athens, 2009), ch. 12.

[32] T. Fotopoulos, "The drift into parliamentary totalitarianism," The International Journal of Inclusive Democracy, Vol. 2, No. 4 (November 2006). http://www.inclusivedemocracy.org/journal/newsletter/vol2_no4_parliament _totalitarianism.htm

[33] Alan Travis, "Britain "sliding into police state"," The Guardian (28/1/2005).

[34] See the Athens weekly Vema on Sunday (6/12/2009).

[35] Ian Traynor, "EC to keep Greece under scrutiny," The Guardian (4/2/2010).

[36] Helena Smith, "Super-rich move billions out as debt crisis overwhelms Greece," The Observer (7/2/2010).

[37] Source: Fitch; Olivetree securities, The Independent (6/2/2010).

[38] V. Georgas, Eleftherotypia (30/1/2010).

[39] P. Arestis & T. Pelagidis, The Guardian (1/2/2010); K. Vergopoulos, Eleftherotypia (29/1/2010) et. al.

[40] K. Moshonas, Eleftherotypia (14/7/2006).

[41] World Development Indicators 2002, Table 2.5.

[42] See T. Fotopoulos, Dependent Development: the Greek case (in Greek) (Exantas, 1985), Table Γ3.

[43] World bank: World Economic Indicators '08, Table 2.3

[44] ibid., Table 4.1

[45] World Bank, World Development Reports 1980 & 1995, Table. 2

[46] "Greek central banker among world's best paid," Kathimerini (English edition) (23/10/2008).

[47] See Takis Fotopoulos, Towards an Inclusive Democracy (London & NY: Cassell, 1997), ch. 6; The multidimensional Crisis and Inclusive Democracy (IJID, 2005), ch. 14 and "Transitional Strategies and the Inclusive Democracy project", Democracy & Nature: The International Journal of Inclusive Democracy, Vol. 8, No. 1 (March 2002) http://www.democracynature.org/vol8/takis_transitional.htm

[48] See T. Fotopoulos, Dependent Development: the Greek case (in Greek) (Athens, 1985).

[49] ibid. Table D1.

[50] Martin Feldstein, "Let Greece take a eurozone «holiday»," The

Financial Times (16/2/2010).

[51] Erik Jones, "Greece's capital account problem," The Financial Times (11/3/2010).

[52] See Dirk Meyer' s Interview to newstime.gr on (8/3/2010).

[53] See T. Fotopoulos, "Elections, crisis and popular trapping," Eleftherotypia (26/9/2009).

[54] Helena Smith, "Super-rich move billions out as debt crisis overwhelms Greece," The Observer (7/2/2010).

[55] See G. Oikonomou, Eleftherotypia (5/2/2010).

[56] See T. Fotopoulos, "Transitional strategies and the Inclusive Democracy project," Democracy & Nature, Vol. 8, No. 1 (March 2002). http://www.democracynature.org/vol8/takis_transitional.htm

Greece: the transnational elite's "one way street"*

TAKIS FOTOPOULOS

The tragic events at the fire-bombed bank, during the recent huge demonstration in Athens against the savage measures imposed by the transnational elite (an "unholy alliance" of the IMF and the EU), constitute neither a "murder," as it was hurriedly declared by the permanently and blatantly lying leader of the parliamentary Junta that governs Greece today (G. Papandreou), nor a "provocation," as the traditional Left permanently characterizes any event that it does not control. It was part of a popular counter-violence[1], within the logic of which it is unthinkable that it would aim at the death of oppressed employees (who had apparently been given a "work or strike" ultimatum by their boss forcing them, as it was reported, to work in a building with no fire safety arrangements and behind locked doors). It was an (obviously irresponsible) act clearly directed against property. Such acts aiming at the property of fundamental capitalist "symbolic institutions," like a Bank, are far from rare in today's insurrections at global level, constituting spontaneous popular counter-violence against the systemic (economic and physical) violence. Particularly so, in a country like Greece in which systemic violence has taken such dimensions, which have led to the transformation of the post-junta parliamentary "democracy"[2] into a form of parliamentary Junta — just one step before the formal suspension of basic human rights provisions in the Constitution. The reasons that could explain this transformation are as follows:

• The effective seizure of power in last October's general election through a fraudulent electoral program which, even if it was somehow related to the usual statist "Socialist" program, it certainly had nothing to do with the opposite neo/social-liberal program of a drastic shrinkage of the public sector, i.e. the sector which the current Chairman of the "Socialist" International (and Greek Prime Minister!) considers to be Greece's "big patient" which led to today's informal bankruptcy. This, at the very moment when even bourgeois international analysts and economists (as well as the markets!) talk about the chronic structural crisis of the Greek economy (which actually constitutes the cause of the systemic bankruptcy and not the public sector which is only a symptom of this crisis).[3]

• The clear contempt of the will of hundreds of thousands of strikers and demonstrators, but also of the demand for a referendum that could, even retrospectively, give some legitimacy to the barbaric measures. That is, the measures imposed today by the local and the transnational elites, simply in order to prevent the bankruptcy of our creditors (German, French, but also Greek banks e.g. the Eurobank of Latsis which is now struggling to conceal its exposure to the risk of Greek bankruptcy![4]), at the expense of hundreds of thousands among the lower social groups in Greece who are condemned, instead, into bankruptcy!

• The almost totalitarian use of the TV channels and especially the state owned ones in order to conceal the popular anger at the systemic violence and to obscure (with the help of well known commissars of the system) the real causes of the crisis for which exclusively responsible are the local (political and economic) elites, as well as the transnational elite, who however are not being forced to sacrifice even a single swimming-pool from the tens of thousands of them adorning their Hollywood-type villas! Instead, the low (compared to European levels) salaries and pensions are slashed, thousands of jobs in the public sector are abolished, the hire and fire culture in the private sector is being institutionalised etc. It was, therefore, the ultimate token of impudence for state TV (ERT), which has become an advertising channel for the promotion of the parliamentary Junta and its leader, to denounce the short "occupation" of its studios by unemployed school-teachers (whom the "socialists" threw to the street in their thousands) as engaging in "anti-democratic dialogue," when, for instance, on May Day all state channels devoted their evening news bulletins mainly in broadcasting cheap patriotic speeches by the "socialist" prime minister and his entourage, whereas at the same time the major international channels (BBC, Al Jazeera, etc.) devoted the corresponding news bulletins mainly to the riots, which the graphic ERT presented as minor incidents, almost at the end of its bulletin!

• Police-terrorism that is imposed supposedly for the "protection" of citizens against "terrorists," anarchists and the like. In reality, police-terrorism has the sole purpose to terrorize the middle classes, who — perhaps the first time in their lives — show clear signs of overcoming the class of professional politicians that have deceived them and their party-puppets in the trade unions. The angry scenes outside Parliament on the day of the general strike, with tens of thousands of demonstrators calling parliamentarians as "thieves" and others repeatedly attempting to storm it, made it clear that this was not one more of the usual peaceful (and therefore painless for the elites) marches, and that the people outside Parliament had nothing to do with the carefree world of the elites inside it (and their media). No wonder the real world outside Parliament was met by the virtual world of the elites with tons of dangerous chemicals, so that the demonstrators and everybody else could take the message about who are the real bosses in present "democracy," who can take any kind of decision against their "subjects" without giving a damn to their expressed will.

• The biggest crime of the parliamentary Junta, however, is the blatant distortion of truth as regards the "one way street" which supposedly the measures imposed by the transnational and local elites represent. On this the "socialist" government had surpassed even Mrs Thatcher, who has invented the term in order to describe the similar neoliberal measures adopted by her government in the early 1980s, who, however, did not prevent a dialogue on them, something effectively ruled out by the Greek social-fascists presently running Greece. Thus, the Greek PM and his acolytes repeat again and again the blatant lie that the brutal measures imposed by the transnational elite is a one-way street for the "salvation" of Greece and that an alternative solution would involve "greater pain for all". In fact the leader of the Greek parliamentary junta, which runs Greece with the help of a herd of professional politicians (the MPs of his own party who —together with the few MPS of an ultra-nationalist party— are the only ones who voted in favour of the predatory measures just in order to secure the economic and social status advantages that their position in the power structure involves) did not have any qualms to declare in Parliament that "he has not heard of any alternative solution" — something that implies that either he is completely incompetent or a crook attempting once more to deceive the people. This is because, as I have mentioned in several articles in this column in the past few months, several leading international analysts and economists had recently shown[5] that it is precisely the supposedly "one way street" which is catastrophic for Greece and not the alternative solution. In fact, even a few days ago, a professor at the University of London[6] supported a solution similar to the one that I proposed from this column[7], that is to say, the solution Argentina followed, following the devastation created by the IMF-suggested measures, which were effectively identical to the ones being imposed on the Greek people now by the transnational elite. And this is exactly the crime committed today by the "socialist" parliamentary junta in Greece, supposedly for the sake of the "general interest" — a nauseating lie which "forgets" that one of the basic socialist principles that gives meaning to the very idea of socialism, is that on matters relating to economic interests, only class interests exist. Particularly so when even leading (bourgeois) international analysts stress that: "Greece is being asked to do what Latin America did in the 1980s. That led to a lost decade, the beneficiaries being foreign creditors."[8]

Yet, even now, this crime of the elite could be terminated, through an intensive struggle, led by the scapegoats of the system in the public sector, aiming at a general strike that would paralyse the State mechanism, and with such demands as follows:

a) An immediate exit from the Euro-zone, so that Greece regains its economic (fiscal and monetary) sovereignty and impose its own conditions on the creditors rather than the other way round, as at present;

b) A re-introduction of the Drachma instead of the Euro followed by a significant devaluation of it (at least 30%) to cover for the continuous appreciation of Euro in this decade, which particularly harmed the most significant Greek export industry, tourism, whereas it made imports from abroad particularly cheap, at the cost of domestic products that they substituted;

c) A conversion of all debt denominated in Euros to Drachmas, so that, on the one hand, creditors could not benefit from the devaluation of the currency and, on the other, debt repayment becomes a complete Greek affair;

d) A renegotiation of debt aiming, first, at a drastic reduction of it (to compensate for the high interest rates already paid for its servicing, as well as for the speculative activities around interest rates in the past and second, at a significant extension of the repayment period;

e) Strict controls on capital movements, so that the huge capital flight by the elites (Greek and foreign) of the last few months could be stopped immediately;

f) Socialization of the Banks, so that no speculation against Greek deposits could take place when the above steps are taken, and all deposits to be guaranteed by the state to be made readily available (up to a limit, say €50,000 per year) so that the elites and privileged social groups are prevented from boycotting the new arrangements by creating panic and inflation;

g) Heavy taxing (after recording/registration) of the major real-estate and mobile property (yachts, luxury cars etc) and forcing those from the local elite and privileged social groups who have already transferred vast amounts of capital abroad in the last few months to pay these taxes on their property in Greece;

Of course, this alternative solution does not mean, as the elites and their media say in order to terrorize people, that the State would stop paying salaries and pensions, apart from confiscating their deposits. I dealt with the issue of deposits above but as regards pensions and salaries, it should be made clear that if the state declares default this does not mean that it would cease fulfilling its obligations to everybody else apart from its creditors. The state would simply stop paying the billions it owes to foreign and local creditors, until they are forced to pay the debt — whose they were the main, if not the exclusive beneficiaries. The above conditions will simply secure the welfare of the people during the transition period to the repayment of the debt and at the same time they would create the preconditions for a self-reliant development that would abolish for ever the need of lending from the market sharks, which has led to the present conversion of Greece into a protectorate of the transnational elite.

* This article is an edited version of an article first published in the mass circulation Athens daily Eleftherotypia on 8/5/2010

LEAFLET: CANCEL HERE AND NOW ALL INTEREST PAYMENTS TO FOREIGN BANKSTERS

Thieves and abusers of public money, highly-paid workshy sub-contractors, kickback receiving middlemen and every type of parasite exists from when the new Greek state was created. These phenomena aren't a Greek peculiarity but are part of and a permanent character of the world capitalist jungle we inhabit. Government and Mass Media of Disinformation are highlighting these side events to make us believe that the crisis isn't of a structural nature, but a simple problem of …bad management, which by devilish coincidence appeared for the whole of the 192 countries of the planet!

Humans produce to satisfy their biological and cultural needs. But under capitalism they don't determine the products of their labour. They hand them over to the market! After, like a religious person seeks salvation in a picture made by a religious artist, current man depends on his luck from the independent laws of the market which he himself created. The market may make him rich or destroy him. It is above man and his logical control.
Today there are in Greece more than 150,000 newly build apartments and many of us are homeless. Fields the size of football pitches with thousands of cars whilst we go about on foot. We walk shoeless whilst around us there millions of pairs of shoes. We are hungry and the market refuses our right to produce. Thus by definition our existence.

The crisis isn't due to overconsumption like the parrots of the power assert but due to the overproduction of goods in relation to the consumer possibilities of society which becomes limited due to unemployment and the pressure on wages.

These aren't cyclical crises like they were in the 19th Century. Don't let anyone believe that slowly or surely the depression will give way to a new boom.

From the last Great Depression inaugurated in New York in 1829 and the human slaughter of WW2 which was masked by 30years subsequently of economic growth, ended up digging further the ditch for capitalism. That is because it was based on the policies of inflationary givebacks, on the basis of an overvalued dollar without gold backing. The result of this is we now have the first combination of depression and inflation. Unemployment with astronomic prices in relation with the crisis of the 1930's where unemployment was accompanied with deflation. Let it become common knowledge: we are living through the worst crisis known in the history of capitalism. A crisis from which there is no peaceful exit. Humanity once more is facing the dilemma of 'socialism or barbarism' either radical solutions will be imposed to today's impasses or the human species will return to caves after some type of nuclear annihilation. There is no third road. The union and political leaderships won't go far repeating in today's pre-revolutionary conditions the same reformist slogans which they had 25years ago. Or something which is the same –replacing- concrete programmatic proposals with loud noises and abstract condemnations of capitalism and words in favour of socialism.

The measures of restricting the buying power of the masses which PASOK and the IMF are taking will lead to a depression in the form of an economic avalanche. They know this but can't follow another path. Their tax stripping measures won't provide anything. You can't get blood out of a stone! The public sector debts will rise to new heights. Every delay in the taking of development measures will cost dearly. The first measure of aid required isn't the bailout of the bankster's but saviour from them by declaring bankruptcy. Not a penny to foreign thieves. They owe us but we don't owe them

Greece takes out loans so as to pay previous ones. This has occurred from the birth of the Modern Greek state. A loan for Kolokotronis in 1823 was paid back one odd century later in 1832. 5 months ago we paid back another loan of the revolution. To receive the recent loan which we won't see a penny (it's just an accounting act) we have been obliged to buy 6 French Frigates and 6 German submarines!

As a people we are paying back to foreign capital $500 billion euros of interest payments alone. Now the international bloodsuckers are arriving to tell us we owe even more. If an end doesn't come to this looting every type of development and exit from the crisis will be a joke.

End the debt payment just like the govt of Iceland did as it got the opinion of its people via a referendum. From 1970 we have had 40 'bankruptcies' and they have generally aided problematic economies. Russia, Argentina and Venezuela have had such 'bankruptcies' basing their economic development, with fast rhythms in the last few years.

May 2010
www.patari.org

Greeks tried to storm Parliament and subsequently the KKE called them 'fascist provocateurs'....

London Solidarity Meeting : Greek General Strikes

Another 24hour general strike occurred today and the KKE-Communist Party excelled itself in its sectarian divisive action propping up Papandreou's government. Instead of marching from Sintagma (Parliament Sq. to Omonia) they marched from Omonia to the Ministry of Labour and then asked its people to disperse walking to Thiseo, the area around the Acropolis which is in the EXACT opposite direction of Parliament... Stalinists see Parliament now like the Dracula sees the cross; they avoid it at all costs as the most impoverished gather there who want the struggle to continue in a militant fashion.

GSEE-TUC with the Eurostalinists Siriza and the leftists of Antarsya marched to Parliament but ensured they continued past it in a rush refusing to congregate there. Thousands remained outside shouting militant slogans:

'Thieves Thieves'

'Scumbags, Traitors, Politicians'

'Send PM George to Goudi (Prison)'

'Take your mother and leave the People don't Want You'

'Unions which overthrow not Submit',

'Here and Now Cancel all Foreign Debts',

'Bread, Education, Freedom, the Junta never died in 1973'

'Send Jeffrey (PM Georges nickname) to the USA'

To the police a section of the demonstrators chanted 'It will become like Argentina', 'Guard those that rob you' , 'Shameless drop down your shields'

When the demo passed outside the Marfin Bank

'Chrisohoidi,(Minister of the Interior) Provocateur, Murderer'

These 24hour token strikes are reaching their historical limits. There is no point in marching 6-8 times to Parliament or from Parliament to fight another day. The leaders of the official left despite the numbers of people involved are working in tandem trying to weaken the resistance and peoples resolve. The economic crisis is becoming clearly a crisis of leadership as the measures aren't going away but will get worse as cuts have now been extended to the private sector, not just the public sector workers according to the latest info from the IMF.

Thu 20, May 2010 @ 23:12
VNGelis said...

The issue of the Euro-breakdown has now gone mainstream in one of the banksters daily, the Telegraph

Whatever Germany does, the euro as we know it is dead

Angela Merkel's ban on short-selling is just a distraction from the horror to come

http://www.telegraph.co.uk/finance/comment/jeffrandall/7746806/Whatever-Germany-does-the-euro-as-we-know-it-is-dead.html

Another interesting article comparing the Tea Party movement in the USA with the Greek labour protests

"Drop Dead Economics": The Financial Crisis in Greece and the European Union

http://www.globalresearch.ca/index.php?context=va&aid=19107

There is also this:

Public Meeting-Counterfire-Conway Hall

Can't Pay Won't Pay-Solidarity with the Greek Protests

Debate: Weekly Worker on EU, Euro & Return to Drachma

Weekly Worker 817 Thursday May 13 2010

Europe and the Greek contagion
The crisis in Greece is bound up with the global capitalist downturn. Instead of a nationalist response there could be an international fight-back, writes James Turley

After eight months of increasingly fervid speculation, the European Union has finalised a bail-out package for struggling Eurozone economies.

And for all the strenuous denials from Berlin and Brussels that such economies - first and foremost, Greece - would not be rescued, the package that has been announced is substantial: firstly, €110 billion to bail out Greece; secondly, €500 billion from EU member-states, all told, and an additional €250 billion from the International Monetary Fund as an emergency reserve for everywhere else.

This is, by all accounts, a spectacular turnaround. The core EU nations have long enjoyed a global competitive advantage through the wide space created by Europe's open market. Germany in particular sustains a massive industrial base, selling to countries like France (10.2%), US (6.7%), Netherlands (6.7%), UK (6.6%), Italy (6.3%), Austria (6%), China (4.5%), Switzerland (4.4%). When the crisis started to bite at the borders of Europe, Germany, France and the rest were equally keen on insulating themselves from the ill effects. The Greek government was told to take the begging bowl to the IMF - and sharpen its already punishing austerity measures.

Alas, for Angela Merkel, the Greek 'contagion' could not be so easily quarantined - after all, Greece is in the euro zone, and will be for the foreseeable future, so Greek problems are also European problems. Any disaster in Greece immediately poses the question: who is next? At which point, the list of EU candidates facing the possibility of their own sovereign debt crisis is growing: eg, Portugal, Spain and Italy.

Exactly how much money rides on the comparatively modest Greek economy at the moment became abundantly clear on May 6, when - with speculation over the Greek situation reaching fever pitch - the Dow Jones plunged 9% in half an hour. The immediate trigger for that collapse is believed to be an error at one particular bank, which erroneously saw an automated transfer of $16 billion (rather than million) worth of shares. Given the increasingly common use of automated trading on the world's stock markets, however, it is significant that a computer glitch could have such harmful effects just now. Market turbulence continued the next day, where the London stock exchange fell significantly - bad news from the continent exacerbated by the inconclusive outcome of the general election.

And so it was that, on Friday May 7, the Bundestag approved its share of the Greek bail-out package, effectively making it a reality. The German government nodded through this enormously unpopular message only two days ahead of an important regional election - another index of the intense capitalist pressure EU states are under to sort this mess out.

Domino effect

This unlikely scenario is the effect of a number of mechanisms. Firstly, the background to the Greek crisis is the accumulation of significant levels of state debt, which was hidden using fraudulent (i.e., astute) accounting practices at the time of Greece's entry into the euro. Euro zone rules stipulate that government budget deficits must not exceed 3.2% and national debt not exceed 60% of GDP; the Greek government, with the collusion of US investment bank Goldman Sachs, hid enough of its bad figures to sneak in. Debt, of course, has to be paid for in interest. As recession bit, tax takings dropped - and financing government borrowing became more and more difficult as interest rates soared. In the case of Greece to 20% and even 38% as the country was rated as a basket case.

Secondly, there is the pervasive influence of financial speculation. With the invention of the credit default swap, one of the many dubious derivatives, it became possible - in theory and, before long, in practice - to profit from the failure of debtors to meet their payments. The flipside to this process is that buying these derivatives in great numbers reflects badly on that country's financial stability, and so the activity of speculators is a self-fulfilling prophecy. At the moment, betting on the collapse of national economies is an alarmingly easy way to make a quick buck.

Throw in the international dimensions of the crisis, and you have a potential domino effect - a Greek default, followed by a Portuguese default, and so on ... which could ultimately lead to a run on the euro. In that respect, it was obvious from the start that the Greek bail-out was not going to be enough - the Greek crisis would not have been half the headache for the international bourgeoisie if it was not simply one aspect of a serious structural crisis in the euro zone. Much more was clearly needed - and the new package appears to have stabilised the markets somewhat.

However much of this bail-out money is actually needed, it is only a temporary solution. That debt has not been paid off, but simply shifted around - the core EU economies, meanwhile, are not in a position to keep pouring money out of their own coffers. The Greek deal, then, has a lot of strings attached; principally, Greek Prime Minister George Papandreou is expected to make budget cuts of an order shocking even to bourgeois commentators.

Exactly how successive rounds of summits and talks continue to find yet more limbs of the Greek economy to amputate is a matter of some speculation; but so, for once, is the question of whether the operation is even possible. On one level, the concern is an orthodox economic one - with austerity measures so harsh, and the cash going straight to creditors, how exactly is the economy ever to recover?

The other side to the trepidation of the bourgeois class is: can this Greek government successfully impose this on this Greek population? Papandreou has been locked into pursuing austerity measures ever since he acceded to power last October - and he is already facing mass resistance. Though the largest union federations, the private sector General Confederation of Greek Workers (GSEE) and the public sector Civil Servants' Confederation (ADEDY), both supported the election of his PanHellenic Socialist Movement (PASOK) mass pressure, in no small part channelled through the

Communist Party of Greece (KKE), has forced the trade union bureaucracy to organise a string of general strikes. The latest, on May 5, coincided with the EU's discussions over the Greek bail-out package. As I write, more protests are planned for this week, with events around the European bail-out fund gathering pace.
The resistance

That the international bourgeoisie doubts Papandreou's ability to defeat the anti-austerity struggles - at least with this latest prescription for social carnage - testifies above all to the well organised and well-disciplined character of the Greek workers' movement. The KKE has not suffered quite so severe decomposition as its more illustrious fraternal parties elsewhere; it remains a significant political force in the unions, and has marshalled that influence into a sustained campaign against what is, after all, a social democratic government. Though it remains an 'official communist' party, and therefore intellectually hamstrung, with the Kremlin no longer issuing orders it is now able to act on its own initiative.

So it has a strategic policy for the working class - a great "people's front" of "the workers, the self-employed, the craftsmen, the small tradesmen, the small and medium-sized farmers, and the young people". It is all these folks' "patriotic duty" to build "our own Greece". [1] Given the source, the nationalism is hardly surprising, and a substantial portion of the blame goes to the EU in the KKE's view. This is a line shared to an extent with groups to its left, which tend also to be flatly opposed to the EU. Antarsya, a coalition of "anti-capitalists" including the Greek sections of the Fourth International (Usec) and the British Socialist Workers Party-dominated International Socialist Tendency, campaigns for an "anti-capitalist exit" from the European Union.

Both arguments are tempered with nods in the direction of internationalism - that the KKE unfurled two huge banners at the top of the Acropolis, reading (in English) "Peoples of Europe - rise up" signals the party's (rather muted) awareness that the Greek crisis is not just a matter for Greeks; meanwhile, Antarsya welcomes "the proposal for coordinated action of solidarity and against the cuts on a European level by forces of the anti-capitalist left and the movements". [2]

The problem is that these two things are flatly counter posed. Firstly, a successful revolution in Europe - that would last longer than months - would have to be a European revolution, covering the whole continent. This, in the last analysis, has nothing to do with the EU - it was true in Marx's time as much as it is true of ours. It does not matter how successful defensive struggles in Greece become; there comes a point where the government has been rebuffed in all its efforts and thereby the question of power is posed, and the Greek workers will be objectively faced with the task of constructing a society in their own interests.

An isolated country - Greece, Britain or any other - would face only wrack and ruin if it attempted to defend workers' rule under conditions of capitalist boycott and resistance and the large-scale flight of capital. Starting the revolution in one place or another then hoping for it to spread elsewhere is a strategy doomed to failure - the revolution can only be a coordinated seizure of power, building upon substantial international organisation.

In this respect, the EU has imposed a certain unity on its member-states - unity of a degree and kind amenable to the capitalist class, of course, but unity of a sort. Our problem with the current set-up, which pitches smaller economies in a radically unequal relationship with the core countries, is not that it is too much unity, but not enough - that is, the core powers attempt to have their cake and eat it, exploiting the structural imbalance of the EU's institutions to profit from the economic links, while retaining an effective stranglehold on political power.

Seizing on the EU as a particularly egregious agent of the capitalist offensive in several countries, the European left has all too readily fallen into advocating models of an "anti-capitalist exit", which are chimeras. The only anti-capitalism capable of superseding capitalism - that is, communism - demands the ever closer unity of peoples. Anti-EU leftism is, at best, a crab-scuttle sideways in relation to this strategic objective rather than a stride towards it; in reality, it can only encourage illusions in 'national roads' to socialism, and is thus a step backward.

The European capitalist class has, in effect, two roads open ahead of it. The first is to restrict membership of the euro to the countries highest up the pecking order in the EU - those in particular who can keep up with Germany. Hardly an attractive option - a great deal of political capital, not to say capital proper, is invested in the current set-up, and paring down the euro zone is not likely to be a painless process for anybody concerned. The second is to centralise economic decision-making, and tighten fiscal controls over member-economies. This amounts, in practice, to handing over even more power to the core countries, and is understandably a hard political sell - both in countries like Greece, which do not appear to have much to gain from continued euro membership in the next decade at least (apart from sustained austerity measures comparable to the crippling regime of reparations imposed on Germany after World War I), and in Germany itself, where the capitalist media often portray Greeks and others as leeches on German prosperity. The bail-out fund, of course, is a move in the latter direction.

The job of the workers' movement is not to choose between these non-solutions - but to press its own policy for the radical reorganisation of society on a continental scale. Dutiful statements of solidarity are not sufficient expressions of internationalism - what is needed are the firmest possible political unity in the battle to replace capitalism with socialism. We should fight for genuine democracy on the terrain of the EU alongside the terrain of our national polities, which are every bit as rigged against us as the Brussels bureaucracy. Against the mendacious advocacy of unity by capitalist states fighting for position in the global pecking order, we fight for an indivisible Europe under the rule of the working class - as a key step towards the overthrow of capitalism throughout the world.

Notes

1. inter.kke.gr/News/2010news/2010-05-05-strike

Greek Left

The article on Greece ('Europe and the Greek contagion', May 13) presents the Greek left as being anti-EU when, in reality, they are committed Europeans who stand candidates in all Euro-elections and take up seats in the European parliament.

Thirty-odd years of EU membership have brought Greece to the brink of bankruptcy. The Franco-German bloc, who runs the EU, presents itself as a benevolent charity, an Oxfam at large, that supports the small nations, develops them and integrates them into a higher, more developed standard. The exact opposite is the case.

Greece was de-industrialised in the last decade. A whole swathe of previously public sector companies have been privatised - e.g., Telecoms, Olympic Airways, etc. Coupled with annual arms budgets in the region of $7 billion annually going to the EU and the enforced investments of billions in the wider Balkan region, we have the small nation attempting to survive while two countries spend over 70% of the EU's budget - Germany and France.

Just as Latin America attempted enforced dollar parity on all the currencies, which ended in tears, so what has started in Greece will spread and bring down the euro, whether we like it or not. The idea, as presented in James Turley's article, that revolution has to be coordinated throughout Europe before it happens, is absurd and goes against the whole history of Europe.

VN Gelis

Coward

It is unusual to see an unsigned article in the Weekly Worker ('Workers' defence', May 13), but seeing the subject matter the cowardice of the writer might be understood.

The tragedy of the deaths of bank workers in Greece is the occasion for a declaration of war by the CPGB (PCC) against anarchism. No matter that no evidence need be provided to prove the guilt of the anarchist movement as a whole or even in detail for this crime. For your anonymous would-be Chekist, it is enough that we exist to condemn us.

I look forward with some interest to the next demonstration when I will expect to see the mass ranks of the CPGB (PCC) workers' defence squad ranged against a skinny white bloke with dreadlocks and a dog on a string.

Darren Redstar

Absurd

VN Gelis thinks the idea of coordinating revolution throughout Europe is "absurd" (Letters, May 20). The comrade even insists that the idea "goes against the whole history of Europe". True, in a way, but profoundly wrong all the same.

All working class revolutions to date have failed. Why? The Paris Commune of 1871 because it was isolated. The 1917 Russian Revolution became the Stalinite counterrevolution within the revolution in 1928 because of isolation. But a revolution in one country undoubtedly impacts on all other countries to one degree or another and results from often deep- seated systemic causes.

Take the year of revolutions in 1848, the springtime of the peoples of Europe. The first signs of those great events were the rumblings of 1846 in France and Poland. But raising its snout first in Sicily and then the northern Italian states, the mole resurfaced in France in February, ending the constitutional monarchy of Louis-Philippe. From France it spread to Germany in March, then Denmark, then Austria, then Hungary, then Poland, then ... Switzerland.

Karl Marx and Frederick Engels had a clear premonition of the 1848 revolutions in 1847. Take a look at the Manifesto of the Communist Party and note that they urgently sought to get it translated into as many European languages as feasible: i.e., English, French, German, Italian, Flemish and Danish.

They certainly believed that the coming revolution in Europe should be as closely coordinated as possible. Chapter four is devoted to the relationship between the communists and the existing opposition parties in Europe.

The First International, of which Marx was the effective leader, was established to coordinate the struggles of the working class. Primarily in Europe ... but also in the United States. The Second International was based on the principle of 'one state, one party', but sought to bring workers together globally through symbolic actions such as May Day strikes and demonstrations. The Third International put the communist parties under firm, centralised leadership ... and adopted the slogan calling for a "United States of Europe" in 1923 at Trotsky's urging.

What is really absurd is not the idea of co-ordinated revolution. It is the idea promoted by comrades such as Gelis who believe that small states such as Greece can escape pending bankruptcy and domination by France and Germany by breaking away from the European Union and dropping the euro. For what? Splendid isolation ... like Albania under Enver Hoxha?

No, the communist revolution is necessarily international because it overthrows international capitalism positively. We take over what capitalism has created. Our revolution might begin in an isolated country. A Brazil, an Iran or a Turkey. But by its very nature it is international ... and the idea of not planning, not consciously directing, not timing that revolution strikes me as either anarchistic or plain stupid.

Enso White
London

Back to drachma

Enso White argues the Greeks cannot break away from the euro, as this will lead to it becoming like Albania (Letters, May 27). Media commentators have argued that, if the Greeks push it too far, a new set of colonels will return. In other words, one first has to wait for the revolution in the UK to break out before resistance and clear demands are placed to the mass movement to cancel the foreign debts and return to the drachma.

Bankruptcy is here in the form of the EU-IMF agenda, which has a two-pronged strategy: to create a depression (GDP collapse in the region of 10%-20%) and to break Greece apart, so that it becomes a region of the EU without a national parliament, national budgets or national decision-making (the Kallikratis plan). All will be controlled from Brussels by some new Euro-Gauleiter ('commissioner' is the latest version of the name).

The Greek resistance to Hitler's occupation didn't wait for the resistance in France or Italy. Resistance occurs whether one likes it or not. The issue is whether one is able to channel it in a proper direction, not allege that if you resist and leave the EU you will become Albania. That isn't an argument, because in recent years Zimbabwe has resisted. So has Iran, so has Cuba and so has Venezuela. They are still standing.

Arthur Lawrence, on the other hand, argues that local struggles cannot break the stranglehold of the most extreme form of EU-IMF dictat, as that would lead to trade wars and barriers - another form of protectionism. So we have to put up with them. This is precisely the strategy of the Greek Left in its attempt to prop up the EU-IMF measures. They gathered thousands on the demos but, when a section of the demo tried to storm parliament, the KKE, in its traditional style, condemned the protestors as 'fascist provocateurs'. Exactly what they did in 1973 with the Polytechnic uprising and in 1944 with the murder of the Guerrilla leader Aris Velouhiotis.

Lenin argued that a capitalist united states of Europe was unrealisable or that it would be reactionary. The euro is dead. It hasn't withstood the test of the crisis. We are just waiting for the funeral to be announced. But it is coming, as day follows night - just like the whole Euro project of integrating the industrial north with the poorer, non-industrial south. Greece has paid $500 billion in interest payments alone in the last decade or so and buys up $7.5 billion in arms annually from the northern Europeans. It now has some of the highest prices, some of the lowest per capita wages and the highest VAT rates, thanks to the EU. The EU is a bosses' racket, but they can keep it. We don't want it.

Next time round, the organised forces of the left will not be able to contain mass anger, as the economic crisis isn't going on vacation. An Argentinian-style popular explosion is on the cards. The Argentinian masses broke dollarization, restored their currency and introduced import controls to defend national production. Any organisation that doesn't have them as their example is pro-globalist and pro-new world order, pure and simple. You will find yourselves directly in conflict with the mass struggles in Greece, just like the KKE has started to be.

VN Gelis
Weekly Worker 820 Thursday June 03 2010

Euro-Breakdown
Whether you like it or not the Euro is in meltdown. Now whether imperialism is dominant isn't the issue per se for until capitalism is overthrown globally imperialism will be dominant. One doesn't put the cart before the horse. We can't expect the world revolution to solve our immediate problems without raising concrete demands not philosophical abstentionism which is the professional stock trade of every Stalinist huckster. There is escape from imperialism and Zimbabwe has shown with its land seizures of white owned farms that it has taken its destiny into its own hands and very soon they are going to take over white owned mines.

Greece has to follow the Argentinian path, restore its currency as a first step and cancel all foreign debts overnight. This is what the situation demands now and all those who don't demand it want foreign creditors paid (i.e. imperialism).

The fact is and they are undisputable that the organised forces of the left (KKE & Syriza) are acting as props to the IMF-EU junta. They march workers like humpty dumpty up to the wall only to march them down again. They have no solution to the crisis other than repeating stereotypes about capitalist boom and bust and whether in the EU or out of it, imperialism dominates. They have been unable despite the numbers on all the general strikes and demos to stop any measures and when the masses act on their own and stay on the streets they will probably re-emerge in their classic role as ministers of some coalition government as they did in 1989. But today there is a big class difference. The crisis isn't going on vacation. Club Med is bust. So is the Euro. So is the Left. What comes next will be determined by living social forces. This isn't a re-run of the 1930's. It will be much worse.

VN Gelis   Weekly Worker 822 Thursday June 17th 2010

Tsipras-Leader of the pro-EU globalist ex-Euro's

Resistance to the IMF

Editor's Note: This series of articles coupled with many eyewitness accounts try to provide a basic flavour of how the Greeks have responded to the IMF-EU-ECB known in Greece as the 'Troika' and the despicable role of the Left mis-leaderships which have squandered opportunity after opportunity...

After the IMF's Arrival the Greek Left in Crisis

The largest demos since the fall of the military junta in the 1970's have led to measures being passed despite the size and militancy of the people in protest. How did this occur and what implications does this have on the future course of developments?

Economic Crisis-IMF Imposed Depression Economics

First we had the Greek bank bailouts to the tune of E28billion then we had the Greek bailout to the tune of E100billion then we had the Euro bailout. Most recent studies speak about a collapse of Greek GDP to the tune of 9%. (1) Construction according to Eurostat has dropped 30% in 2009 and going on towards 50% for this year according to the Greek media leading to an exodus of many immigrant building workers to neighbouring Balkan countries and the press reports about 200,000 apartments unable to be sold. Retail outlets are closing daily and rents have been generally reduced between 10-20% due to lack of business and many parts of Athens now look like a war zone with many boarded up shops which once they go unrented remain thus. Hotel bookings are down by 12% so far and when this accounts for 20% of GDP this will affect the economy even more and unemployment has now officially hit around 11%

So the questions that now exist are will Greece fare better within the EU or outside of it? Two recent studies debate this, but the fact that the anomalies of the EU are hidden from most studies is illuminating. Greece pays annually E10 billion in arms purchases of which 50% go to two countries, France and Germany. It also contributes annually E4billion to the EU. Alongside that it has made annual investments to neighbouring Balkan countries since the fall of 'communism' to the tune of E1-2billion annually. Its agricultural products are now re-sold back via French and German owned supermarkets at higher prices in Euros than in Paris or Berlin. Its interest payback for Greek bonds has increased to 8% annually up from 4%, whilst VAT has gone up to 23%. With low average wages these massive hikes in the cost of living will affect workers standard of living as inflation is currently at around 6% and wage freezes have been announced for 3 years. Coupled with the pension cuts, to avoid a depression will be an economic miracle worthy of a Houdini.

Studies:

http://www.guardian.co.uk/business/2010/jul/11/european-debt-crisis-germany-euro
http://www.guardian.co.uk/business/2010/jul/07/breakup-emu-eurozone-deep-recession
http://epp.eurostat.ec.europa.eu/cache/ITY_PUBLIC/2-28062010-AP/EN/2-28062010-AP-EN.PDF

Construction

http://epp.eurostat.ec.europa.eu/cache/ITY_PUBLIC/4-19052010-AP/EN/4-19052010-AP-EN.PDF

The arrival though of the IMF has occurred for a purpose. Putting Dracula in charge of a blood bank one cannot expect him not to drink it. Already we have hospital cuts, closures, chaos as government contracts with suppliers enter a totally new phase of non-payment and already reports have appeared of ambulances having no petrol, hospitals having no bandages or gauzes and operations being postponed indefinitely. Behind the new deal to be agreed in hospital contracts will of course be the hidden hand of global pharmaceutical companies who are after Greece's small but important for its people, hospital sector. More privatisation and sub-contracting will be the outcome.

KKE Strategy-Capitalism isn't Collapsing, Divide and Rule of Workers Movement

6 General Strikes each one becoming smaller in size than the previous one, nearly every six weeks has been the sustained action against the IMF-EU imposed austerity measures.

Having controlled the union federations of more than 50 unions and having taken a decision to not participate in the Greek TUC more than 5 years ago (as it is a sold-out leadership according to the KKE) they call their own general strikes at the same time as the Greek TUC, but at different locations in Athens. The purpose: to avoid workers unity in action, i.e. on the streets.

The large demo on May 5th where members of the KKE union federation PAME attempted to storm Parliament, led to a breakdown in control. The numbers on the demo were impressive, the measures hadn't really passed by then and the KKE leadership assumed that the crisis wasn't necessarily going to be as severe as was being reported, but working people were expecting the worse so they turned out in numbers. They joined the KKE demos en masse in a series of demonstrations, 5th May and on 15th May. But after that the KKE deliberately attempted to march away from Parliament and go towards the Acropolis and the backstreets of Athens. Why would they do this? They have historical form. Whenever movements swelled which they could not control, by sailors in the 1970's against the re-structuring of shipping crews by ship owners, building workers in the 1980's and farmers throughout the 1990's due to reductions in CAP and agricultural imports, they sold out the people concerned.

Whenever they do their best to demobilise resistance by ensuring it is divided into separate demos, separate days, even separate hours on the same day, the govt of the day starts a massive attack on the KKE alleging it is about to …launch the revolution. This provides it time to pretend to its members internally that they are on the right political path and that everything is ok. But the problem remains. The measures announced by the IMF-EU dictat speak for themselves. 3 year pay freezes, 50% cut in redundancy payments, across the board cuts in pensions ranging from anything from 10 to 30%, increase in VAT to 23% etc. and these measures aren't going away, however much the KKE adopts the ostrich approach pretending that they are provisional and a new upturn is round the corner, which will stabilise the situation in favour of the working class.

Split in Syriza-Sinaspismos (Ex-Euros in death agony)

Having become synonymous with the youth protests a couple of years earlier regarding the cop killing of a teenager, Synaspismos (Coalition of the Left) recruited around 13 far left groupings ranging from Maoists to Trotskyists it assumed that the only way was up when it had identical policies to the KKE but just of a different order. Instead of marching with the KKE it marches in the demos held by the Greek TUC and ADEDY (public sector unions) closely followed by the grouping around ANTARSYA. As a consequence of the repeated strikes and sensing some splits were likely to occur in PASOK (as some MP's voted against the government and were booted out) a faction around Kouvelis (and historic old timer ex-leader Kyrkos) split taking 5 Parliamentary deputies with him forming the Democratic Left. Their positions are to support solutions to the IMF-EU imposed cuts within the confines of the EU and to not seek to demand departure from it or to even raise the possibility of abandoning the Euro which is gaining ground amongst many people.

15th June-General Strike-Eyewitness Account-2010

With the backdrop of strikes by sacked Olympic Airways employees who surrounded the Ministry of Economics after the selloff to a bank (Marfin whose CEO is Vgenopoulos, the bank that led to the death of 3 workers) and strikes for a couple of days previously of Metro workers (due to unwarranted sackings of staff), the KKE gathered in Sintagma to march to Thiseo (area around the Acropolis) and GSEE gathered in-front of its building to march to Sintagma.

On this day the KKE had the largest banner ever seen on a demo which hang from the lights in central Athens, so large in fact they had trucks which specialise in lifting furniture into high rise buildings into congested areas and what they lacked in terms of militancy they achieved in terms of clinical efficiency. They set up shop, gave the same old speeches about victory being around the corner and they disappeared in record time, less than an hour just in case workers met at Sintagma from the other demo on the other side of central Athens. Having started their speeches by 11am they had left the square by 12pm no doubt having spotters at the Greek TUC demo just in case unity was achieved at this late hour. Let's not forget that the week before the KKE held a mini- general strike all on its own and only 5 odd thousand turned up, when on the 15th May it must have had over 100k. The main slogan of the KKE 'People Don't Kneel Over, the Only Path is Resistance and Struggle' sounds militant but it is more about themselves as a leadership, than people in struggle.

The union leaders who were addressing the sacked Olympic workers who hadn't received their redundancy payments and were refusing to disperse around the Ministry of Economics just off Syntagma square were told in not too many words by a screaming union official that he is going out of his way trying to get their agreed settlement and that if they don't like it he will go home as he doesn't need this type of stress of people calling him names. The same groups of fired workers in previous general strike had thrown rotten eggs at the union leaders calling them 'scumbag union sell-outs'. Union leaders have to work overtime in this period and they aren't happy as they have nothing to offer the workers below, not even crumbs. Hence their divisive, splitting, sectarian, disorganising tactics now come to the fore in broad sunlight literally.

Why have two separate demos for over a three month period? What is the purpose of it? The old slogan of 'workers united will never be defeated' no longer allegedly applies. Despite the remaining demo arriving in Syntagma sq. from the Greek TUC building the leaders of the demonstration wanted it dispersed as quickly as possible but a few thousand remained outside Parliament chanting slogans and booing at the MP's who appeared at its windows intermittingly. At the front of the steps of Parliament were a group of workers from the Greek shipyards sold off to ThyssenKrupp one of the main backers of Hitler's Third Reich. They were stating they hadn't been paid for months for work carried out there. This has not been forgotten even for the servile media which started to speak about a 4th Reich…

A small section tried once more to storm the steps but the police fired tear gas and repelled. At another section of the demo a Greek protestor was spotted with a Greek flag and was allegedly accused of being a 'fascist' (same policy the KKE used previously) and was chased by gangs of youth. The police saw the disturbance and tried to intervene in the middle of the crowd provoking a counter-disturbance and a new round of tear gas was fired creating mini-mayhem.

Argentinian style social explosion against the IMF will be the outcome

Having been placed under the direct rule of a Triumvirate EU-IMF-Central Bank the infamous Troika as it is called in Greece the role of the national politicians becomes more limited as they months go by. Despite organising another general strike 10 days later which took the exact same format as before just the starting and finishing locations being different and with a lot less people, it is becoming clear to most people that this style of struggle has reached an impasse. The impasse is political instead of doing with demoralisation. The organised forces of the left have done everything in their power to demoralise the resistance without proposing anything other than 24hour token strikes, which are monotonous in both speeches and the organised sloganeering.

Both sections of the opposition (KKE-Synaspismos) have made big hue and cry over workers who wanted to go further labelling them 'fascists', 'provocateurs' etc. and not limit themselves to the confines of the traditional form of protest as they understood the government was hanging the sword of Damocles over its MP's and threatening them with new elections and de-selection if they didn't vote the measures through. A weekly newspaper associated with PASOK Paron.gr has predicted a very hot autumn despite the 159votes of the governments MP's for the IMF austerity package. They note indeed that these MP's have disappeared from public life as a day doesn't pass without one of them being confronted in public by people who are incensed by the cuts being pushed through and the general depressive economic climate.

June 2010
VN Gelis

Eyewitness Account: The Greek Left at an Impasse

The most recent figures point to a 9% fall in Greece's GDP. Unemployment has now officially hit around 11%. Construction has fallen 30% in 2009, according to Eurostat, and the press reports it is heading towards 50% for this year. About 200,000 apartments cannot find a buyer.

An exodus of thousands of immigrant building workers to neighbouring Balkan countries is underway.

Shops are closing daily and rents have been generally reduced by 10-20% due to lack of business and many parts of Athens now look like a war zone with many boarded up shops. Hotel bookings are down by 12% so far and since tourism accounts for 20% of GDP this will affect the economy even more.

The crisis has sparked a debate over whether Greece would be better off outside the EU. While most attention is given to the "help" that Greece is getting from the rest of the EU, little is said about just how much Greece is ripped off by the rest of the EU. Greece pays €10bn a year in arms purchases of which 50% go to two countries, France and Germany.

It also contributes €4bn a year to the EU. The country's agricultural products are now re-sold back via French and German owned supermarkets at higher prices than in Paris or Berlin.

The interest payable on Greek bonds has increased to 8% annually up from 4%, whilst VAT has gone up to 23%. With low average wages these massive hikes in the cost of living will affect workers' standard of living as inflation is currently at around 6% and wage freezes have been announced for three years.

Already we have hospital cuts and closures. Chaos is rife as government contracts with suppliers enter a totally new phase of non-payment. There are reports of ambulances having no petrol, hospitals having no bandages and operations being postponed indefinitely.

Behind the new deal to be agreed in hospital contracts will of course be the hidden hand of global pharmaceutical companies who are after Greece's small but important hospital sector. More privatisation

and sub-contracting will be the outcome.

The Left's Failure

Greece has experienced six general strikes during the current crisis, each one smaller in size than the previous one. The leaders of the unions are responsible for this state of affairs.

The KKE controls the federations of more than 50 unions. Five years ago it took a decision to not participate in the Greek TUC and ever since prefers to call their own general strikes at the same time as the actions of the Greek TUC, but at different locations in Athens. The purpose: to avoid workers unity in action, that is, on the streets.

The large demo on 5 May, when members of the KKE union federation PAME attempted to storm parliament, led to a breakdown in their control over the rank and file. The numbers on the demo were impressive; the measures hadn't passed into law by then and workers felt they could stop it from happening.

Although the KKE leadership assumed that the crisis wasn't necessarily going to be as severe as was being reported, working people were expecting the worst, so they turned out in large numbers.

They joined the KKE demos en masse in a series of demonstrations on 5 and 15 May. But after that the KKE deliberately attempted to march away from parliament and go towards the Acropolis and the backstreets of Athens. Why would they do this? They have a history in this area. Whenever movements swelled which they could not control – by sailors in the 1970s against the re-structuring of shipping crews, by building workers in the 1980s, and farmers throughout the 1990s fighting against reductions in CAP. In each decade of struggles the KKE sold out the people concerned.

On each occasion the KKE does it best to demobilise resistance by ensuring it is divided into separate demos, on separate days, even separate hours on the same day. s

Syriza-Sinaspismos (Ex-Euros)

Having become synonymous with the youth protests a couple of years ago after the cops killed a teenager, Synaspismos (Coalition of the Left) attracted about 13 far left groupings ranging from Maoists to Trotskyists.

Its politics are not so different to those of the KKE. Instead of marching with the KKE it marches in the demos organised by the Greek TUC and ADEDY (public sector unions).

As a consequence of the repeated strikes and sensing some splits were likely to occur in PASOK (some MPs voted against the government and were booted out) a faction around Kouvelis split taking five parliamentary deputies with him to form the Democratic Left.

Their positions are to support solutions to the IMF-EU imposed cuts within the confines of the EU and to not seek to demand departure from it or to even raise the possibility of abandoning the Euro which is gaining ground amongst many people.

29th June General Strike – Eyewitness account

The latest general strike took place against the background of protests by sacked Olympic Airways employees who surrounded the Ministry of Economics after the airline was sold off to a bank as well as strikes a couple of days previously of Metro workers (due to unwarranted sackings of staff).

On the day the KKE gathered in Sintagma to march to Thiseo (area around the Acropolis) while the GSEE gathered in-front of its building to march to Sintagma.

The KKE had the largest banner ever seen on a demo which was so large in fact they had trucks which specialise in lifting furniture into high rise buildings to get it aloft!

They set up shop, gave the same old speeches about victory being around the corner and then they disappeared in record time, less than an hour, just in case workers from both demos met at Sintagma.

Having started their speeches by 11am they had left the square by 12pm, no doubt having spotters at the Greek TUC demo just in case unity was achieved at this late hour. Let's not forget that the week before the KKE held a mini- general strike all on its own and only about 5,000 turned up, whereas on 15 May it must have had over 100,000.

The union leaders addressed the sacked Olympic workers who hadn't received their redundancy payments and were refusing to disperse from outside the Ministry of Economics just off Syntagma square.

They were told by a screaming union official that he is going out of his way to try to get their agreed settlement and that if they don't like it he will go home as he doesn't need this type of stress of people calling him names.

The same groups of sacked workers in a previous general strike had thrown rotten eggs at the union leaders calling them 'scumbag union sell-out merchants'. A small group of protestors tried once more to storm the steps of parliament but the police fired tear gas and repelled them.

Union leaders have to work overtime in this period and they aren't happy as they have nothing to offer the workers, not even crumbs. Hence their divisive, splitting, sectarian, disorganising tactics now come to the fore.

Having been placed under the direct rule of a Triumvirate, EU-IMF-Central Bank, the role of the national politicians becomes more limited as the months go by. After organising another general strike on 8 July which took the exactly the same format as before but with a lot less people, it is becoming clear to most people that this style of struggle has reached an impasse.

The impasse is not because workers are demoralised. The organised forces of the left have done everything in their power to dissipate the resistance by proposing nothing other than 24-hour token strikes, which are monotonous in both speeches and the organised sloganeering.

Both sections of the opposition (KKE-Synaspismos) have made big hue and cry over workers who wanted to go further, labelling them 'fascists', 'provocateurs' etc. for not limiting themselves to the confines of the traditional form of protest.

A weekly newspaper associated with PASOK Paron.gr has predicted a very hot autumn despite the 159 votes of the government's MPs for the IMF austerity package. It's imperative that the cycle of smaller and divisive protests ends so that renewed struggles can reverse the defeats suffered so far.

Mon 12, July 2010 @ 22:47

Discussion of this article

Andrew Burgin said...

'Greece has experienced six general strikes during the current crisis, each one smaller in size than the previous one,' Is this correct I thought the high point was the General Strike on the 5th May?

Wed 14, July 2010 @ 22:50

VN Gelis said...

Yep since the 5th May which was the high point. So technically my statement is wrong. But the KKE also held a rally on 15th which was massive where they tried to rally the troops and keep them corralled into their new line of fighting 'fascists' who tried to storm Parliament on the 5th. This alienated all the new supporters that rallied to them so by the end of June when they held a mini-general strike on their own only around 5k turned up. They then avoided the totally go it alone tactic and joined the general strikes called by the Greek TUC but from a different part of Athens. Since the 5th they have also marched to the Acropolis and avoided Sintagma. Indeed on 29th June they told their most active members to create human chain around Parliament facing towards the crowds, just in case anyone tried a repeat of 5th May.

Thu 15, July 2010 @ 20:00

Whatever Happened to the Struggles-Interview for PR

How do you assess the results of the last six months of strikes and protests against the government/IMF cuts packages? Has the government been forced to modify, delay or abandon any elements of the austerity drive?

The demonstrations led to a mass explosion of workers' anger. The general strike on 5 May for the first time led to conflict between the base of the KKE (Greek Communist Party) and its followers who were carrying PAME flags (their trade union body). This was the high point which was cut short by the government's provocation against the Marfin Bank workers. [1]

In reality the only people who are hoping for some sort of solution are the international banks who have received many times over the amount of capital they have loaned. To understand how Greek debt has accumulated one must remember that six months ago Greece re-paid a loan which it had received during the revolution of 1821!

The Greek government is taking out loans to pay back previous ones and as a result the foreign debt now stands at €325bn and about another €50bn will be added to this in 2010. Meanwhile, public debt amounts to 120% of GDP and instead of getting smaller will rise to around 150% by the end of 2010.

The government will be obliged to proceed to take even harder and more vicious austerity measures. It won't abandon or change its policies. It is not intimidated by a series of 24-hour strikes and demonstrations; in essence a number of street parades at a safe distance from the centres of power.

Why did the trade unions fail to intensify the protests beyond one-day strikes as the summer progressed? Wouldn't an indefinite strike of transport and the public sector have brought the government down? Was it that the rank and file were not prepared for the sacrifices of an extended strike, or were the leaders of the trade unions too fearful?

The reasons for the failure are political. The Greek TUC leaders who are generally known as "godfather workers' leaders" are political appointments which lead to their top chiefs eventually entering Parliament or some other type of state subsidized NGO. With such a career path mapped out they never want to rock the boat. The other union leaders associated with the KKE, under the umbrella known as PAME, split from the Greek TUC more than a decade ago and refuse to march together with the TUC. Despite the numbers on the demos and general strikes, no unified action was ever achieved in any general strike. We arrived at the ridiculous situation after the 5 May strikes whereby the KKE refused to go near the centre of the city and marched to the tourist spots of the Acropolis in order to disperse.

After calling their own supporters "fascists" for attempting to storm Parliament, the KKE held a mass rally on 15 May where at least 200,000 gathered and where the usual Stalinist policy of escalating the fight in the not too distant future was announced; but the actual outcome was division, disorganization and dissolution. On the one hand they refuse to strive to overthrow capitalism; on the other, they refuse to call for Greece to leave the EU – and so provoke an Argentinian-style default – since they argue that capitalism will still dominate the country.

In practice therefore their policy is to strengthen the position of the KKE and their unions and little else; they have done everything in their power to keep the workers' movement divided and disunited. The rank and file showed its militancy at the 5 May demo when thousands occupied the steps of Parliament to demand that the "thieves were prosecuted" and that the "politicians are forced to pay". With this action the rank and file instinctively realized that the traditional one day token strikes were leading nowhere.

Without a united workers' response – joint demos, joint disruption of capitalist functioning (as happened during the lorry drivers' strike) – the 24-hour parades only have the effect of demoralising large groups of workers as the crisis of leadership becomes a crisis for the whole of the class. They could at least have organised a blockade of the IMF offices in Athens or called for the surrounding of Parliament to not allow the MPs to leave, or even for camps to be set up outside Parliament, something that would rally the people to the cause.

Instead the forces of the left demoralised and disorganised the resistance, by assuming that the methods of yesteryear (a general strike every so often followed by a march) would guarantee some type of crumbling of the will of the politicians.

How do you assess the economic situation going into next year? Recovery or further recession and worse?

In the April-June period this year Germany experienced a strong recovery but Greece's recession deepened. Tourism is down at least 15% from last year. Building construction (which represents 25% of GDP) has gone into free-fall down by at least 33%. Unemployment according to INE-GSEE (Greek TUC's Labour Economic Institute) is scheduled to hit the one million mark by December 2010, that is, about 20% of the workforce. Thousands of shops which are not part of large chains are closing daily – an estimated 17% so far of 3,500 outlets. The centre of Athens is starting to resemble a post-industrial war zone.

There is much petty crime, drugs are traded openly in broad daylight and at night the centre turns into an area where there are very many street prostitutes.

The IMF packages aim to speed up the sackings of workers to aid in the continued privatisations that have been announced in the train companies and the national electricity system which to date have remained under state ownership.

The full liberalisation of a whole host of middle class professions: hauliers, black cab drivers, pharmacists, solicitors, lawyers etc. aims to allow big companies to take over these sectors and turn the staff into salaried employees. That way they can increase productivity, and profits with lower costs possible to the consumer and other businesses.

One has also to take into account that in Greece social security payments for the unemployed only last one year and in order to qualify one has to have worked a full two years. After that there is nothing.

The consequent fall in consumer spending and the increase in taxes (e.g. an across-the-board VAT rise to 23%), the rise of official inflation to 5.6%, coupled with the short term increase in interest rates on government bonds (8%) and the three-year imposition of zero wage increases in both the private and government sector, point in one direction only: a collapse of GDP and therefore the tax base of the government.

This is guaranteed as it is impossible for Greece to export its way out of the crisis while it is a member of the Eurozone and paying the punitive rates of interest to foreign bond holders. In the first six months of 2010 there has been a 4% fall in GDP so if this continues through to the next six months we could be looking at around a 10% fall.

When will the major social effects of lower pensions, benefits and pay really bite? Will this force people back onto the streets?

The demonstrations this year occurred essentially prior to the measures being taken in order to forestall them. As such one can say the struggle was generalised before the crisis really started to bite across the board. One cannot predict what is going to happen next or when a new strike will provide a spark for a generalised anti-IMF insurrection. But no one, including the mass media, is predicting calm waters ahead; instead, everyone is waiting for a storm.

The wage freeze, cuts in pensions and mass sackings in the public sector, the looting of the population, the collapse of social welfare and the stopping of public works, does not only make people despair but it intensifies the crisis of the market and make the recession tip over into a full blown depression.

When people are condemned to a level of poverty in which thousands upon thousands will go hungry, the state threatens to sink itself. Where is the government going to generate the increased tax revenue it requires to fulfil the demands of foreign creditors?

Can you say something about the role of education sector, the role of students during the last wave of strikes? What role will students play in the September/October period in relaunching generalised struggles?

Mostly adults were on the demos against the IMF. Students and university students, whilst taking part, haven't been involved in their own occupations against the IMF measures. Very many joined either the Greek TUC or KKE-PAME organized demos.

Due to the pension attacks about 12,000 teachers in primary and secondary education have asked to receive their pensions and quit their job. This has created a shortage of 20,000 teachers when schools open again in September. The government has announced it will only recruit another 3,000 leaving a massive shortfall which will be covered by compulsory overtime of between 5-10 hours for each teacher. And this is happening alongside reductions of between €1,000-€3,000 a year for every teacher.

The enforced transfer between primary and secondary schools or vice-versa to cover shortages is also one of the Presidential measures passed. Women teachers will be hit by the retirement age being raised to 65. So the attacks on women and students are among the most brutal of the IMF-government measures.

So when the summer holidays are over students will return to schools without many teachers, with an increase in the remaining teachers' workload and with the latter having a big hole in their pay packet. Taking into account that youth unemployment has already reached about 40% for all young people between 18-25, a whole generation are never going to have a reasonable chance of a job so probably see no point in studying.

Have any parts of the far left grown in the course of the strikes and demonstrations? Has Pasok suffered a major loss of support?

Many workers who had either voted for PASOK or the other big parties rallied to the KKE during the demonstrations. The demonstration of 5 May was definitely the biggest ever since the fall of the military in 1974. There must have been more than 800,000 present – the centre of Athens was jammed, people could not march anywhere as the roads were full. After the IMF measures PASOK politicians have had difficulty going to restaurants or appear in any public place.

Middle class professionals confront them in almost daily tirades such as, "give back the stolen money" and "pay our restaurant bills". Almost always the police are called to "restore order" after various things are thrown at the politicians such as ashtrays, salt and pepper pots etc. But only 3 PASOK MPs have jumped ship.

The only real growth that occurred in the left was thousands joining the KKE contingents on the demonstrations, but this was before being called "fascists". This slander has provoked internal conflict, leading already to splits in one section of the official left (Synaspismos-Syriza, the ex-Eurostalinists). But this growth had more the character of participating in the demonstrations as opposed to people actually becoming members. Yet the large number who occupied the steps of Parliament chanting "thieves, scumbags, politicians" shows that they are ripe to go further than the existing political and trade-union leaderships will sanction.

The indefinite Greek hauliers' strike which crippled the economy for seven days at the end of July was a spark that was about to light a more general fire. Twice in mass general assemblies' truckers voted to continue their strike. No parties of the left either called for or led solidarity demos in support of the hauliers. The hauliers' union – behind the backs of its members – called off the strike for fear of it leading to a full blown national crisis in the middle of the summer season. The KKE sent a representative who gave a typical trade union bureaucrats speech of supporting the strike on paper but in practice it did nothing to aid them.

[1] This was the incident where three bank workers died when their bank was set on fire during a demonstration in May

VN Gelis
July-August 2010

The Latin-Americanization of Greece and the lessons for the European South*

TAKIS FOTOPOULOS

At the beginning of February 2010, the European Commission (EC) announced plans for Greece which were characterised by The Guardian, with the usual British kind of understatement, as "the most intrusive scrutiny of an EU member state's fiscal and economic policies and book-keeping ever attempted", while the Commissioner himself stated, "this is the first time we have established such an intense and quasi-permanent system of monitoring" --a system that involved a stiff regime of quarterly reports from the Greek government on progress towards fiscal probity and the right of the EC to order extra action, if needed. That was followed, a month later, by the announcement (made by the Papandreou government on behalf of the EC) of swingeing spending cuts and huge tax rises hitting the lower social groups. These measures involved, in a nutshell, shaving off a month's salary from the already low (by Eurozone standards) incomes of people employed in the public sector --who are estimated to be about one million, i.e. 20% of the total labour force-- squeezing of public spending, rises in indirect taxes including VAT, freezing of pensions and worsening of social security conditions with respect to pensionable age, privatisations etc.

The severe cuts in civil servants' salaries and in public spending, which will be complemented by the indirect negative effects on incomes (through the multiplier effect), would bring about, according to Deutsche Bank's predictions, a decline in the GDP by 4% this year alone, whereas the total decline of GDP during the implementation of the program in the next three years would be in the range of -12% up to -20%. The inevitable effect of these predatory measures will be an increase in poverty in a country --which (together with Spain) is the joint record holder of poverty in the Eurozone-- with almost 20% of the Greek population, being on the margin of poverty, struggling to survive. Furthermore, unemployment will become massive, as the dismantling of the productive structure, brought about by the opening of markets since the country' s joining the EU, will be complemented now by the effective dismantling of the public sector. However, as the public sector traditionally played a significant role in absorbing the excess labour within the country, the effects on unemployment would be drastic. The combination of poverty and unemployment, with the uneven effects of the increase in indirect taxes on low incomes, will further increase inequality, one of the highest in the EU. The inevitable result would be the creation of a number of wealthy oases for the rich (locals and foreigners), in the midst of huge deserts of poverty concentrated in monstrous urban conglomerations --exactly as it happens in similar cities all over Latin America at the moment.

No wonder that the announcement of the measures have created a huge "river of anger" that poured in the streets of Athens and other major cities in repeated general strikes and sometimes violent demonstrations. Particularly so, as it is more than obvious that the measures announced will neither catch the enormous tax evasion, nor shall they force repatriation to the country of the 10 billion of Euros or so, already escaped abroad in the last couple of months since the crisis was announced, to be added to at least 60 billion Euros which had already fled the country! However, had these funds and the local wealth been subjected to a drastic proportionate extra property tax (something which is of course inconceivable for the elites), the famous debt problem could have been solved in a flash, without having to beg for new loans from the foreign elites, which (with profit in mind of course!) have been imposing onerous conditions that the future generations will have to pay for many years to come. This, despite the fact that it was the same elites and privileged social strata (local and foreign) who created and primarily benefited from the debt and the growth 'bubble' it led to.

The predatory measures imposed on Greece by the Directorate of the EU, expressing the Eurozone's political and economic elites, clearly give the impression of a complete colonisation of the country by the transnational elite. It is, obviously, one thing to implement similar measures by a formal consensus of the people (as in Britain, Holland, Sweden, etc.) and quite another to enforce compliance with such measures, as it happens now in Greece. Particularly so, when these measures do not have any popular legitimacy, given that the ruling "socialist" party was elected a few months ago on a program that provided for policies entirely different from those imposed now on the Greek people. This, despite the fact that the leadership of the ruling party was fully aware of the economic crisis --which is basically chronic-- and deliberately deceived the electorate, with the help of the political and economic elites controlling the mass media, which were keen to have a "socialist" party elected as the only one capable to implement such measures because of its comprehensive control of trade union bureaucrats.

The fact that the economic crisis is chronic is expressed by the post-war dismantling of the production structure, which was brought to completion with the opening of its markets to the world market --a process that was accelerated by Greece's integration into the EU at the beginning of the 1980s. The effective dismantling of the productive structure, in turn, inevitably led to the creation of "a consumer society without a production basis" and a continuous growth of the external debt, and consequently of the public debt that has presently exploded. Naturally, these developments did not --nor could they-- lead, anyway, to the formal bankruptcy of the Greek state, as this would have opened huge holes in the pockets of German and French holders of Greek state bonds and would put at risk the stability of Euro itself. Particularly so, when other countries in the European "South" face similar problems --i.e., what the capitalist markets call the "PIGS" (Portugal, Italy/Ireland, Greece, Spain). However, the price to be paid, particularly by the lower income strata (workers, employees, under-employed, unemployed and pensioners) in the coming years, will be very heavy indeed. No wonder the measures were presented by the media, in a massive brainwashing campaign, as unavoidable, something which is true only if we take for granted the present institutional framework of today's capitalist neoliberal globalisation, namely, the open and liberalised markets, which are the ultimate cause of the crisis along with the consequential treaties of Maastricht, Lisbon and the Stability Pact.

In this context, competitiveness, (which depends on low wages and employers' contributions/taxes, high productivity, price stability, etc.) plays indeed a crucial role with respect to an exporting economy that bases its development on the free movement of commodities and capital (like Germany or China!). The Euro, therefore, cannot be separated from the Stability Pact, as is hastily suggested by the reformist Left, because --in the given institutional framework-- it is only when the common currency is complemented by criteria like those prescribed by the Stability Pact that monetary stability and the competitiveness of the advanced capitalist countries in the Eurozone can be achieved. In other words, the policies of squeezing wages, prices and budget deficits, are necessary for the EU economic elites to be able of surviving in the competition with the corresponding elites in USA, China, etc.

But, if such policies are to the benefit of countries like Germany, which played a leading role in the design of the Euro, they are in no way beneficial to countries like Greece, Spain, or other countries in the European "South". Thus, it is true that the policy of "hard euro" and the consequent policies of squeezing wage costs had led to a significant improvement of German competitiveness and consequently of the German balance of payments which, starting with a deficit of 1% of GDP in the Balance of Payments on Current Account in 2000, achieved a huge surplus amounting to 5% of its GDP today. It is also true that, in the same period, the labour cost in the European South has risen faster than in the North and that in countries like Greece and Spain the increase in labour costs, faster than in Germany, has led to the decline of their competitiveness and has consequently worsened their balance of payments (Greece's deficit tripled in absolute numbers and Spain's increased by as much as six times, etc.). --which ultimately led to an increase in the public debt to finance the bubble of "growth" that Greece or Spain had enjoyed since their adoption of the Euro.

Yet, this does not mean that to avoid surpluses in the North and deficits in the South all countries in the Eurozone should follow the same policies of squeezing wages and salaries. One should not forget that, historically, wages in the South were (and still are) almost half of those in the North (e.g. the minimum monthly wage in Greece, Spain and Portugal in 2006 was less than half of that in the European North). Therefore, implementation of such policies throughout the Eurozone would simply lead to further divergence between the North and the South rather than to convergence, which is supposed to be a main aim of EU and the EMU! In other words, a real convergence in wages and salaries would have led to such huge differences in competitiveness between the European North and the South that no transfer of funds from a new institution (like the proposed by the reformist Left European Monetary Fund) would have been capable to eliminate. This is why a real convergence within a capitalist market economy has not been achieved even within single capitalist nation-states like Italy, Germany, UK, etc., let alone a monetary union like the EMU!

So, the problem with the EU and the EMU is neither their "lack of solidarity" towards a member state, nor the policies of "hard Euro" followed by the European Central Bank and the German and other elites, as the reformist European Left suggests. The real problem is the EU and the EMU themselves! As it could be shown by both theory and historical experience, in any economic union consisting of members characterised by a high degree of economic unevenness (as is the case with the EU), the establishment of open and liberalised markets for commodities and capital would inevitably lead to a situation where those that primarily benefit from the free movement of commodities and capital would be the more advanced regions/countries (which have already developed high productivity levels and advanced technologies) at the expense of the rest. It is not therefore surprising that, historically, none of the presently advanced capitalist countries --which are now keen to promote the freedom of trade, etc. -- opened its own markets before it had already achieved a high level of competitiveness for its own exports, under protected markets.

It is, therefore, imperative that the anti-systemic Left, in Greece and in Southern Europe in general, directly challenges the present European integration in terms of markets and capital, and fights instead for the establishment of a new confederation of European peoples, initially in the European South, where they share common economic, political and social problems. This is a first step towards the creation, in the future, of a new institutional framework which institutionalises the equal distribution of political and economic power among South European peoples, and among all citizens within each part of the confederation --a development that could serve as a model for the integration of European peoples as a whole, within a pan-European confederation of Inclusive Democracies. This implies the elimination of power structures and relations, which characterise the present so-called "democracies" and capitalist market economies, and their replacement with new societies where the peoples directly, and not through "representatives," control the political process, as well as the economic process through the collective ownership and control of economic resources, within a framework of self-management by workers, peasants and students of factories and offices, farms and education places respectively, in a way that reintegrates society with Nature.

Pensioners have suffered the greatest so far in the first wave of IMF measures....

Economics of the EU and Greece

What has been sold by leftists and globalists who stand for the EU is that it is a form of charity which helps the small countries of the EU.

As the chart below shows Greece contributes the most as a percentage of its income to the EU.

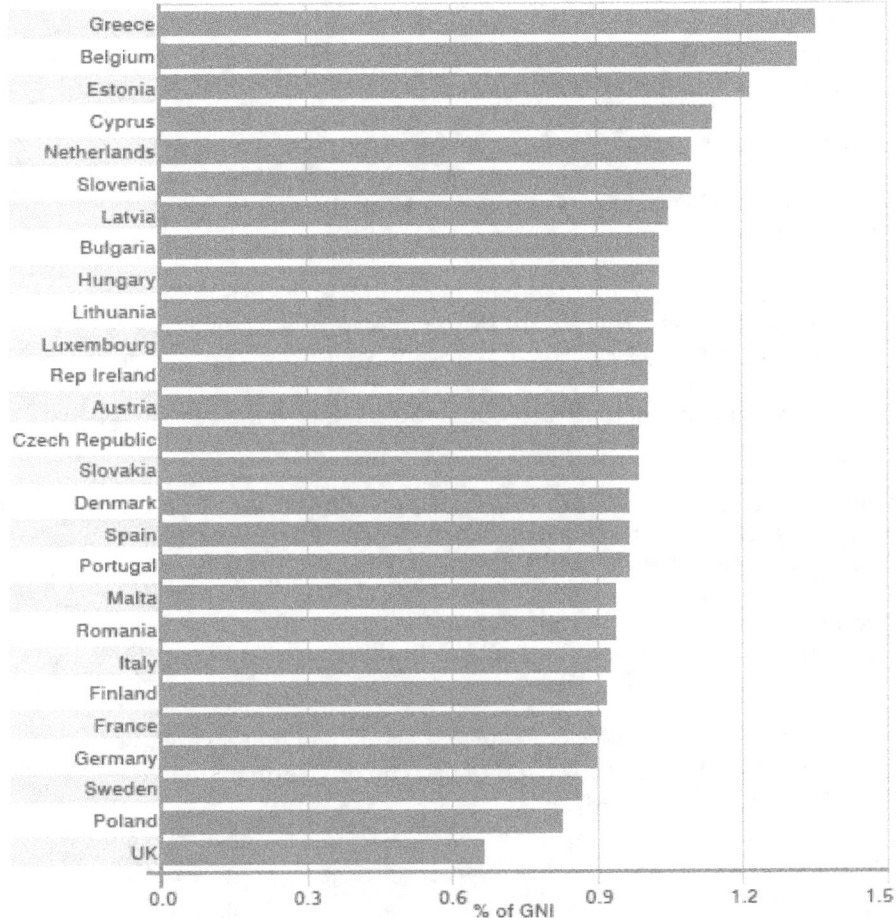

The entire 'surplus' it receives goes straight into agriculture which is then for export to the northern industrialised countries which can't grow enough food for their populations.

Hence the volumes of fridges produced by Germany have a higher net value than what is produced by agriculture in Greece.

Greece therefore received absolutely zero from the EU and props it up.

On paper Greece is a net receiver of EU funds to the tune of E8billion whilst contributing E4billion.

Greece, the EU's highest military spender between 2000 and 2005, finally realized the cost of military purchases to its economy and decided to curb its military spending.

Greece bought 4% of all arms sold in the world in the past five years. Greece buys 31% of its arms from Germany, 24% from the US, 24% from France and 21% from other countries.

Turkey's military spending gradually declined and fell to $11.6 billion in 2008, while Greece's military spending consistently increased, reaching $9.7 billion in the same year.

http://www.todayszaman.com/tz-web/news-201848-arms-purchases-to-count...

CAP was supposed to secure indigenous growth first i.e... Europe first but instead the Eurocrats have allowed imports to cripple European agriculture. The losses incurred in this run into billions for Greece.

Therefore 3 decades of membership of the EU have ensured Greece goes bankrupt and is looted dry, but a globalist with no maths or economics states the exact opposite.

Factor in the 3 million illegals that work just to send money home, implies the land of Greece is used to prop up the Germans and the French and their industries.

VN GELIS

Debate with PR on the Nature of the Crisis...
The Eurozone after the Greek bailout

The Greek sovereign debt crisis briefly threatened the existence of the Euro itself. The response of the European financial authorities with the establishment of an overwhelming€750bn European Monetary Fund, based on the model of the IMF, has qualitatively accelerated Eurozone integration. Rather than the extensive development of the Eurozone, with the acceptance of ever wider and more marginal members into it, like Greece formerly and Turkey possibly, from here on in there will be and has been a qualitative advance of the pace of the European integration towards the formation of a European state. Capitalism advances by crises. And the threat of a Lehman style melt down advanced European integration further in a day than in the previous decade....writes Bill Jefferies

Karl said...

How will a deepening of the EU be sold in Britain, which is not even part of the Euro? This crisis has brought all the contradictions of the EU to a head; I think the entire projects future is in question.

What about nations like Serbia, which are being asked to comply with some EU requirements in order to become part of the EU? Will these processes now be in question?

My crystal ball sees only problems ahead.

Tue 11, May 2010 @ 13:03

Bill j said...

Certainly I think that new candidates are much less likely to be admitted now. The deal was sold as France - in favour of deepening - against Germany - in favour of expansion. Deepening won. From here on in, candidates will face much more stringent conditions. In fact it's likely they simply will not be accepted at all. Let's not forget Greece fiddled the books to guarantee their entry. They won't want that happening again. But national governments have surrendered their right to set their budgets to the new European fiscal authorities. That is a major step towards the establishment of a single European state.

From threatening the break of the EU the crisis has in fact strengthened its integration.

Tue 11, May 2010 @ 15:17

Greece's Euro Entry

The mythology that Greece had something to gain from entry to the Euro is indeed a mythology perpetrated by the capitalist media. 11 years in the Euro and Greeks are now faced with pre-war conditions of labour rights and wages which will soon reach Egyptian levels if the cuts continue unabated seems to show what, that fiddling the books leads to bankruptcy? This reinforces the central myth of the EU that it isn't a vehicle for big business, but some form of benevolent charity, an OXFAM whose central role is to help the smaller nations, when in reality the smaller nations are faced with national, economic and political annihilation. For EU integration cannot proceed apace without political integration. If one no longer has control over ones economy, politicians are defunct.

If one takes a long term view of history, not the narrow one presented in the article above, the $1trillion bailout with 25% of it being by the IMF implies strings will be attached. The Structural Adjustments programs which made the IMF synonymous with depression politics eventually leading to war and collapse has arrived in Europe for the first time, not via the back door, but in the front. For the IMF conditions in Greece are secret as they are for the whole of the EU.

Up until now we had bank bailouts now we are essentially having state bailouts. The issue now is who will bailout all these bailouts. The next phase of the crisis, will lead to dislocation, disruption and the unraveling of the EU. They bought some time for now...

Bill j said…

What are you on about? The article is all about the strings attached. OK I appreciate you've your own spin on things, but why not at least read the thing your slagging off?

Tue 11, May 2010 @ 20:25

Vngelis said…

The world's capitalists were never likely to repeat the mistake again.

Bill J

I did read your piece. Wall Street 1929 occurred in the USA. The second leg of the crash hit European defaults. This recent $1trillion bailout is about what precisely?

A sign of the crash continuing or solidifying European integration? So whilst Vienna was the culprit way back in 1931 and Athens today, in what precise way will bond yields return to pre-bailout times? Default is postponed for now, but like the sword of Damocles it hangs above capitalism.

Tue 11, May 2010 @ 23:01

Vngelis said…

IMF measures in Rumania will take effect soon, strikes called.

http://www.romaniantimes.at/news/General_News/2010-05-12/8612/_Teachers_announce_general_strike

Estonia about to join the bankrupt EURO... as well.

The endless myths circulated in the capitalist media have been that Greece has the lowest average pension age in the whole of Europe. Also the highest pensions in proportion to previous incomes. 1 in 2 British people are economically inactive in their 50's. Economic inactivity in the UK is around 25% of the working age population a figure which is double the actual whole labour force of Greece combined (around 4 million)

The minimum wage will drop from around 670E to 560E.

Average pensions are around 500-600E without a housing benefit component included.

Unemployment pay can only be received for a total of 6 months if someone has worked for 2 years steady. Then one has none. Unlike once more the northern European states which have various forms of benefits which are re-branded but essentially serve the same purpose: unemployment pay.

Hence EU monetary policy for Greece is to strangle it, block all means of survival of the nation and turn them into pariahs in their own country by breaking it apart (Kallikratis plan) so it becomes an EU region, run by some EU commissioner somewhere...

Thu 13, May 2010 @ 09:28

Vngelis said...

If one looks at the EU budget and Greece.

Greece pays the highest proportion out of any state of its income into EU coffers.

It now has the highest VAT rates which go to EU coffers.

It apparently is a net recipient of around E8billion whilst contributing E4billion. The extra E4billion is for CAP.

But such figures don't factor in the $5billion per annum spent on weapons to two EU countries, France and Germany.

Whilst France and Germany spend 70% of the EU budget they also allow tonnes of agricultural imports to flood the EU markets thus destroying Greek agriculture yet this wasn't the reason for joining the EU. Then it was sold as supporting domestic products first over imports into the EU. That was forgotten as usual.

Investments made by the Greek state stolen from Greek pension funds into the 'stabilisation' programs of the EU into the neighbouring Balkan states, the propping up of Albania proper via the presence of around 1.5million Albanians in Greece isn't also factored into any of the Enron style accounting systems of the EU. So as to show that Greece is a net recipient not a net contributor propping up France and Germany they turned accounting on its head and are presenting the Germans as those who sustain fiscal discipline and aren't responsible for the bankruptcy of Greece but the Greek working class.

Heard that one before, in the place of the EU commissioner, place the Gaulaiter and you see history repeating itself. First time round as tragedy, second time round as farce...   Fri 14, May 2010 @ 12:47

Chris S said…

The marxist economist Hillel Ticktin spoke to Yassamine Mather about the Greek bail out and what it means for capitalism in Weekly Worker today: http://cpgb.org.uk/article.php?article_id=1003942   Thu 20, May 2010 @ 13:42

Bill j said…

So what does it mean for capitalism? It's far from clear from Ticktin's article. He says that capitalism cannot solve its problems in which case its crisis is terminal. He also says that capitalism's crisis is not terminal, in which case it can solve its problems. Perhaps it's just fair to say that capitalism can have its cake and eat it...   Thu 20 May 2010 @ 15:45

...If we want to move beyond generalisations like the working class will have to overthrow capitalism in order to achieve socialism, surely what we really need to know is, what will the depth of the crisis be? How will this affect the Eurozone? Will it mean the breakup of the EU? Can the Greek working class resist the cuts? etc.etc.. As far as I can tell Ticktin does not answer a single one of those questions. In which case one surely has to question that value of an article which purports to do just that?

Thu 20, May 2010 @ 23:22

VNGelis said...

No crisis in history is terminal for it only takes another form one way or another. As a social system capitalism is on its way out whether we like it or not.

Capitalism can 'survive' if it forces generalised open slavery on everyone. The market is king, but the emperor has no clothes. They told us the bailouts would solve the banking crisis and here we two years later back to the future. The FTSE has now fallen to below 5,000 which are where it was in October 2009 at the onset of the bank bailout, the currency has been devalued by 25% and an RBS banker on the front page of City AM states that despite the $1trillion Euro bailout, we are on the verge of Great Depression Mark II. Is that happening?

Is the Euro bailout using historical analogies the collapse of the Austrian bank in 1931 that further weakened global capitalism last time round, or is the Euro bailout manageable? The markets will decide, they are king, but the workers won't become direct slaves, they are king. Let's see how this impasse resolves itself by fighting to stop the crisis being dumped on us on behalf of the banksters, the corporate media and the corporate politicians...

VNGelis said...

Of course it's possible that the Eurozone will collapse and there will be another bout of recession. But how possible is it? Not too possible I think, given the scale of the bail out and the experience of Lehman's failure

Bill J

I subscribe to Lenin's maxim on this one. For a Capitalist United States of Europe to exist it either has to be a reactionary formation or unrealisable.

Ex-Chancellor Kohl stated in a public meeting to Germans as reported by ex-UK ambassador Christopher Meyer that the EU is in the national interests of Germany, pure and simple. The project of the 3rd Reich has therefore now morphed into a new 4th Reich with the same implications as before. We cannot have monetary union which doesn't morph into full-blown economic and political union. In order to have the other two therefore national parliaments have to be abolished or lose any political rights when setting economic policy.

The bailouts have failed. Unemployment continues to increase in both the US and the Eurozone as a whole. There are obviously variations on the amounts, but the IMF has entered Europe for a purpose. To impose depression economics, pure and simple. Anyone saying the opposite is covering for them...

Sat 22, May 2010 @ 14:50

Euro unlikely to last five more years...

http://www.dailymail.co.uk/news/article-1284462/Euro-hits-new-low-economists-predict-break-5-years.html

Was the German buyout of E Germany the reason for the current malaise? While losing more than a million inhabitants, East Germany benefited from 1.5 trillion euros of investment since 1991, and much if not most of this has been financed by "foreigners" (non-East Germans).http://voxeu.org/index.php?q=node/4180

So did this amazing amount of money benefit West Germany?
http://ecommerce-
journal.com/news/16736_german_debt_may_top_2_trillio...Here Germany
is the 5th highest...
http://www.optimist123.com/.shared/image.html?/photos/uncategorized/d...
Here Germany's central govt debt has gone from $690 billion in 1999 to
$1.6billion a decade later.

http://stats.oecd.org/Index.aspx?DataSetCode=GOV_DEBT

What was it in 1989?

According to this report what has happened net financial assets are minus
in relation to net fixed assets when both were in surplus in 1990...In this
report on page 8 we see what?

Bundesbank report states govt to debt ratios were 40% up till 1999, they
then increase to around 70% because of unification. The Euro therefore
was Germany's response to the crisis of swallowing up E Germany.
http://www.bundesbank.de/download/volkswirtschaft/mba/2010/201004mb
a_...

Fri 21, May 2010 @ 12:35

Eyewitness Account: Greek Hauliers on Indefinite Strike Against IMF Decrees

On 8 September Greek hauliers held a truckers' march into the centre of Athens with their horns blowing. They were reacting to the decision of the Minister of Transport two days earlier that he has reneged on an agreement made to end the August strike that outlined a transitional period of reforms of the Hauliers terms and conditions of employment. He now insists on the immediate implementation of all the changes without negotiation. As the scene is set for a resurgence of the strike in August we publish here an eye-witness account by V N Gelis of last month's strike and the role of the union leaders in ending it.

"You are taking our livelihoods not simply our licenses" became the battle cry of 35,000 Greek road hauliers who launched an indefinite strike which lasted a whole week before its sell out by its leaders.

When the hauliers met for their mass meeting in the Peroke Theatre in central Athens their despondent voices were heard from one wall of the theatre to the other. They characteristically wore a black armband and came to hear the President of the Federation of Georgiatos who wanted to tell the crowd the proposal of the Minister Reppas that "dialogue will continue only after the cessation of the strike". They forced the leaders to continue the strike...

They rejected the government's plans to open their service up to multinational competition. It was common knowledge that the multinational COSCO which bought the Greek ports on behalf of China asked for 30,000 new licences for transporting goods with Chinese personnel who will be paid a maximum of €300 for their work.

They tried to find a "compromise solution" but their proposals were ignored by the IMF who now essentially runs the Ministry of Transport.

The leaders of the union asked for the pensions of hauliers to reach the amazing amount of €680 a month, to allow for three years for the law to be implemented and not backdated to last June, and the implementation of it for all hauliers to be over a five-year period not a three year period as 5,000 hauliers bought their licences recently and the 35% drop in their value will affect them disproportionally.

New licences were bought for around €300,000 a 35% drop will mean they are now currently worth €200,000 but the debt will remain at the amount for which they were bought.

The Minister of Transport Reppas replied with so-called development tax rebates and allowing each driver to take another licence which will not be worth anything anyway. Even if the majority of the Federation wanted to announce the ending of the strike under these circumstances of a mass meeting with all present, it was impossible as there was nothing on the table.

The KKE's representative at the Peroke theatre greeted the leadership of the hauliers without raising a single point of difference with the government plan despite being self-labelled as the "class struggle union"

So how did the union leaders get around selling out the strike? Four or five days into the strike after two mass meetings and two large demos to the Parliament – and with trucks also parked on many motorways up and down Greece – the government brought forward an "emergency order" which basically allows the military to act as strike-breakers.

This has only been used once or twice before since 1974 against port workers in order to break their strikes. This was the perfect excuse the union misleaders needed to sell out the strike. Why?

Supermarkets had mass shortages of goods. In two supermarkets I visited they had run out of the basics seven days into the strike. There were many fuel shortages in petrol stations. Hospitals couldn't get supplies. More importantly the tourist industry was going to get crippled which is Greece's main earner in the summer months.

Whilst the hauliers appeared on TV stating no one can force them to go to work and they won't accept the provisions of the "emergency order". Army conscripts were also heard to voice reservations that they didn't want to act as strike-breakers. This could pose bigger problems for the government in the future as without the army on your side you lose the ability to threaten people.

So sensing this situation could get out of control, where people in other occupations joined this strike against the IMF and its PASOK quislings, the union leaders met behind closed doors one fine Sunday morning and then the media announced the ending of the strike.

A strike was sold out without being actually defeated and it showed it was a spark that could have lit a more general fire, but the union leaders and the parties of the Left were found wanting once more.

Thu 09, September 2010 @ 13:50

Greek Hauliers have started an indefinite strike again. They are alleged to have attacked the president of northern Greece's CBI during the Thessaloniki trade fair. Their sell out president condemned the violence of the Hauliers but not the violence of the riot police who teargased them.

A video of the event has appeared in this paper.

http://www.ethnos.gr/article.asp?catid=11424&subid=2&pubid=29520948

Sun 12, September 2010 @ 18:48

Hauliers Strike Update...

Blockades have occurred on national motorways and many demos in various cities over the last week.

Lamia was cut totally off in the centre. Different things are occurring in different parts of the country.

Truck drivers act against the line of the union sell-outs.

Much will be decided as to whether people will rally to the autonomous movements of haulier's blockades and whether this will take some organised form or will provisionally go backwards.

Hauliers have started blocking the motorways without a general plan of action. In every blockade autonomous groups are being created under which they decide to go against the official union policy of Tzortatos & Co.

In the Metamorphosis blockade an area on the outskirts of Athens they decided to block both sides of the motorway and at the same time allowed cars to go through the pay tolls by occupying them and allowing them to go through for free.

Truckers have also called for open mass meetings with all the layers of workers and pensioners affected by the IMF measures in the Haidari blockaded which was voted for unanimously. They announced their decision using mobile phones to other truckers around the country, and they want them held at their union offices on Tuesday 12th September 2010

They have also forced scabs to stop working and the one of the union leaders has condemned this via the mass media. Kiousis who owns 35 trucks (and with the 'liberation' of the profession will want to acquire more) attacked the strike breakers under the guise of the 'right to work'. Alongside him was the Hauliers Leader-Tzortatos owner of 17trucks who under pressure of the deranged and corrupted journalists of the IMF mass media pressurised him to support the strike-breakers.

This evening on SKAI TV it was reported that in 3 blockades they are also proposing in the open mass meeting to be held on Tuesday to have all night camps outside of Parliament and to call all the people with them and to not leave until victory.

Sun 19, September 2010 @ 17:28

Strike-breakers on this video showing their demobilised trucks after strikers cut off their electrics.

http://www.megatv.com/megagegonota/summary.asp?catid=17632&subid=2&pubid=13636752

The vote for the 'opening of the professions' one of the IMF imposed measures is going to occur on Wednesday. The KKE hasn't called for any direct support to the Truckers or any of their mobilisations although they are holding a demo outside Parliament on 23rd September when the vote is to go through.

If the truckers march into the centre of Athens with 2,000 trucks as some have stated they will then the situation may go out of control of the union misleaders.

At the same time the President of the Greek CBI has stated that 5,000 containers are blocked at ports all over Greece and much produce may go rotten.

Sun 19, September 2010 @ 19:08

Video of strikers trying to block scabs plus map of all the road blockades around Athens.

http://www.megatv.com/megagegonota/summary.asp?catid=17632&subid=2&pubid=13636752#toppage

Also how the strike is affecting the market with tonnes of stock remaining in the ports

Sun 19, September 2010 @ 19:28

Greek Truckers rally outside Parliament

Greece: truck driver's blockade centre of Athens to halt liberalisation measures

After their union leaders tried to bury the resistance of the truckers in July a new wave of strikes erupted in defiance of the threat of emergency decrees being issued to truckers. Some 19 points around Athens have been blockaded by trucks. Waves of militant rank and file truckers have demobilised scab trucks by blowing their tyres or cutting their electrical connections, so demobilising the engines. The government has tried everything via the mass media to condemn the militant truckers; they even tried to impede the road blocks but it became pretty impossible to stop truckers with 20-plus tonne trucks with engines revving and threatening to squash puny police cars. In the end the police escorted the truckers into various points around Athens – that is, opened the roads for them.

Ta NEA (daily organ of the Lambrakis press - the biggest establishment paper) condemned the actions of the police and demanded to know why the government not confronting the truckers? "Are they allowing them to get away with everything until they get tired and go home?" In the meantime 6,000 containers are stranded in the ports and their perishable contents rot. More stuff arrives daily and has nowhere to be parked.

3,000marched in the afternoon to parliament and the police for the first time in the last 10 years refused to teargas them - which has been standard policy. The reason is clear. They are frightened to attack since they fear provoking more generalised conflict. All train workers of the national railways OSE have also walked out early for a week's strike against ta court decision which tried to deny them the right to strike. So having camped outside parliament on Tuesday night the truckers are waiting for their numbers to swell prior to Wednesday's vote which aims to ratify the IMF's agenda of the full liberalisation of middle class professions, hauliers, taxi drivers, solicitors etc.

If the truckers manage to bring trucks to the centre of Athens and confront the parliamentarian IMF quislings then they may bring about the defeat of the government. The big disaster is the role of the Left once more. Not a single big organisation – the KKE or the Euros Stalinists – have sent as many supporters as they can to support the truckers. 50 members of PAME marched along the pavements in 'solidarity' with the truckers and then dispersed. They have called for rallies against IMF imposed price rises (VAT rates, electricity, water etc.) AFTER the vote in parliament takes place. Divide and rule is the only strategy of the union misleaders. Unifying struggles and supporting the middle class hauliers now they are under total attack isn't for them.

If the truckers are defeated, then the door will be open for many other professions to suffer the same fate. Either which way the government is relying on the politics of the union misleaders to remain in power and appear strong. In reality they are weak and in hiding. The ball for the moment is not in their court.

Wed 22, September 2010 @ 13:55

You would think Truckers would be the first people socialists would want to win over to the struggle as they can literally bring the system to a grinding halt.

Wed 22, September 2010 @ 14:11

The KKE condemned the politically backward ...truckers for using slogans which essentially bring Greeks into disrepute. The media asked the union misleaders of the truckers to condemn the slogans. The slogans were allegedly used by the hooded 'anarchists' no one saw who burnt the workers alive in the Marfin Bank provocation according to the TV station Mega...

The slogans were: 'Repa (Minister of Transport) Go fxxx Yourself', 'Down with the PASOK Junta', 'Air Air get rid of the Cholera', 'Repa you Cxxx we will Enter Parliament'

The Democratic Left a split off from Synaspismos/Euros supported the IMF liberalisation measures during the Parliamentary debate. Synaspismos gave a verbal speech in support of the truckers but like the KKE refused to call out its members in solidarity demos in support of the truckers.

After all night blockade of Parliament and three attempts at breaking through riot police lines, the truckers lost the vote in Parliament. They will now lose the value of the licences of their trucks and many will lose their trucks to banks as the multinational companies that set up new truck companies will bypass them.

Throughout the whole of today they have continued the blockades around Athens.

Their Coordinating Strike Committee has vowed to continue the road blockades until Friday 24th September when they said they will have a mass meeting to work out whether they will continue the struggle. Whilst the railway workers of the national rail network OSE are in their 2nd day of their 5 day strike their union misleaders ensured that they did not march to the centre and meet the Truckers.

Now the liberalisation of transport is law by definition the riot police have to break the blockades. The power of the truckers is in the blockades. If they hold out they can continue to cripple the Greek economy. If they don't, it may imply that each section of Greek society may have to go through the Argentinian path which allowed the IMF to run riot for a full 4 years prior to a social explosion by all the disaffected sections of society led to 9 different governments, the cancellation of foreign debt payments and a return to the peso.

Wed 22, September 2010 @ 20:21

Agree with AA. I think this is a very positive development.

It shows that despite the frequent betrayal of union leaders the truckers have the power to organise their own action and it is a power that through paralysing the economy has the power to bring down the capitalists if the truckers open their mass meetings to the wider working class and take on the questions of the wider working class transforming the legitimate sectional (and important) demands of the truckers' livelihood to the wider issues of the working class- who rules? the bankers, IMF and EU with their austerity? Or the workers who can plan a society and economy based on democratically planning human need, against the need for any cuts, for a workers' revolution to seize the land, the factories and the wealth currently in the grip of a small elite and have a society run by working class people ourselves.

If anything remotely like this is going to happen the left and the wider working class movement needs to rally to the truckers' side, opening up the wider questions of class politics and full heartedly supporting the truckers' strike, instigating solidarity action connected to wider class demands- for workers' control, for an emergency workers' budget to respond to the crisis, the immediate cancellation of all foreign debt, emergency taxes to pay for the crisis- full employment for workers at union rates- including massive wealth taxes and expropriations to take through the workers' demands.

Thu 23, September 2010 @ 05:34

VN Gelis said…

The problem is that not all sections of society have the power to bring the capitalists to their knees. If nurses for instance went on an indefinite strike patients would die and the state would save some money in terms of operations, pensions, dole money etc. The rich go private so they wouldn't care. The issue is also political.

The KKE alleges it is a working class party but has become pettybourgeoisified over the decades. Truckers historically have been on the political 'right' i.e. petty owners, with bank debts and the false consciousness that they will at some point own ten trucks and just collect money from managing them. One of the positives of this struggle is that they have no connection to the dead weight of stalinism and have shown originality in their approach and their sloganeering. They called for an open mass meeting at their union headquarters inviting pensioners groups and other transport workers. But because the union tops are stalinists and they see unity of the workers and the middle class which they can't control like Dracula does with the cross, it was too little too late this time, but it shows the intentions and the possibilities for the future.

The absence of the official Left and the far left is indicative of the extent of the political crisis now the real first wave of struggle against the IMF occurred. It also shows their political direction. Historic leaders of Sinaspismos who left to form Democratic Left have openly sided with the IMF. The next wave of struggle will force the KKE to do the same, as more and more sections of workers and middle class are forced to the streets due to the cuts and privatisations that are continuing unabated.

Thu 23, September 2010 @ 10:26

Jason said…

"One of the positives of this struggle is that they have no connection to the dead weight of stalinism and have shown originality in their approach and their sloganeering. They called for an open mass meeting at their union headquarters inviting pensioners groups and other transport workers. But because the union tops are stalinists and they see unity of the workers and the middle class which they can't control like Dracula does with the cross, it was too little too late this time, but it shows the intentions and the possibilities for the future. "

I think that's key as also is the idea of workers' action committees to unite different sections of the working class (and indeed impoverished or under attack petit-bourgeois, small business owners, traders, owner-drivers etc. who the workers need to win to their ranks).

"If nurses for instance went on an indefinite strike patients would die and the state would save some money in terms of operations, pensions, dole money etc."

Yes but that's why it's essential to have other methods of action to supplement strike action, mass blockades, occupations, different section of workers coming out in solidarity action and can include emergency cover under democratic workers' control during the dispute. It can include workers, students, service users and wider community occupying the factories, offices, schools and hospitals and carrying out production for social need.

Thu 23, September 2010 @ 19:35

VN Gelis said…

Truckers have voted to continue their strike against the IMF

Battles occurred in Piraeus (main port next to Athens) where they blockaded it and the riot police got involved.

The strike committee was flooded with enraged truckers who demanded in opposition to the proposal of the union misleaders to have a secret ballot to have an open air one. The slogan which emerged to the news people was 'we will not give in' Molon Lave (which is what the Spartans said to the Persian Army) in reference to the governments 'emergency orders'.

http://webtv.antenna.gr/webtv/watch?cid=i07je7_i_dp_j_e%3d

The official Left continues to be spectators of an unfolding drama. They chose to have rallies about the price rises and the liberalisation of energy prices instead of supporting the truckers blockades

http://www1.rizospastis.gr/page.do?publDate=24/9/2010&id=12604&page No=8&direction=1

Fri 24, September 2010 @ 20:56

VN Gelis said…

Where are the leftist organisations? Who during their 'insurrection' regarding the murder of the young student Grigoropoulos a couple of winters ago marched up and down streets blockaded police stations, burning down shops?

Why don't they now go to support the Truckers blockades to encourage them?

To help them blockade the roads once and for all indefinitely? When the truckers were outside Parliament all night and tried 3 times to storm it why didn't they turn up?

Why don't they go even outside the headquarters of the GREEK TUC-ADEDY-PAME (union federations) and pressurise them to call an indefinite general strike of all the nation on the side of the truckers for the overthrow of the IMF imposed junta?

Groups and organisations and people are judged in times of crisis when battles hang by a thread. The persistence of the truckers without a single media outlet supporting their cause, without a single political party proposing a solidarity demo, without political representation in Parliament is indicative of a whole generation of politicians both from the 'left' and right.

Fri 24, September 2010 @ 21:16

Fri 24, September 2010 @ 21:16
Jason said…

I think you're right to sharply criticise the left on this. Obviously the Stalinists' leaders are fearful of real workers' action anyway but what about the Trotskyist and anarchist left? What about rank and file workers? I know little I am afraid about the Greek left.

What is it do you think that lies behind the lack of support? Is it because of prejudice against petit-bourgeois truckers? Is there a bad relationship e.g. have sections of truckers not supported workers?

Whatever the past or the explanation it seems to me that this is a crucial dispute. Truckers like railway workers have the ability to paralyse the movement of goods. The working class should pile in behind the struggle, support the truckers' demands, oppose the austerity measures, demand democratic workers' to set prices and get ready to paralyse the whole economy by demanding an emergency workers' budget and plan, nationalise the banks, expropriate the capitalists, appeal to rank and file soldier and police to refuse to break up demos and follow the orders of emergency workers' action committees not the orders of the bourgeois government.

Sun 26, September 2010 @ 22:20

VN Gelis said…

The anarchists have been absent for around a year. Their last great showing was over the death of the banker's son Grigoropoulos whom the media labelled as an …anarchist. Since the IMF arrived they have been absent from all social struggles. Most of the far left, maoists, trotskyists have become part of the ex-euros around Siriza/Sinaspismos in order to get government subsidies which are paid when a party gets more than 5% of the parliamentary vote.

Truckers haven't generally gone on big strikes as far as I know, I only ever remember a big one in the 1980's but agreement was agreed quite quickly. This one now has gone on for a month and previously two weeks at the end of July. There are still 6,500 containers in the ports and many areas haven't had sewage emptied as trucks empty it due to the antiquated system. Many islands have many shortages and much of the fresh produce has gone to waste.

The truckers are voting again today and they are being manoeuvred into having a closed ballot by their union misleaders, instead of a show of hands, so the ballot boxes can be manipulated. Every trick in the arsenal of government unionism is being used to end the strike with the latest argument being that the market needs two weeks to recover, so why not stop now and starts again before things get really serious.

The three other groups (SWP, WRP, Mandelites) who never joined the Euros have refused to support the truckers. At the same time all week strikes have occurred in the trains and now the buses have started as well. So taking into account the KKE has influence in both unions, coordination again is zero, the purpose being to dissipate the anger across different sections of transport workers to prepare them for ...privatisation.

Tue 28, September 2010 @ 20:28

VN Gelis said…

The vote just came through from the Strike Committee, 74 to 6 to continue the strike. Their leader refused to say which way he would vote prior to the vote, but made a statement that whichever way the vote goes he wants all sides to support it.

Tue 28, September 2010 @ 20:55

VN Gelis said…

A 41 year old trucker died after being tear gassed at the blockades of the port of Piraeus a couple of days ago. He was buried today. He is the first victim of the IMF imposed liberalisation of truckers' licences. The union leadership have produced no statement regarding his death.

Greece has been threatened by the EU if it does not issue new truckers licences and the government is processing a new sub-law which states that all truckers who refuse to move their trucks from the blockades will be imprisoned immediately for 3 years, removal of licences and taking over their trucks if they have deliveries for the public sector e.g. hospitals or schools. One trucker on a road blockade on the Athens-Corinth motorway has been imprisoned already.

The Greek TUC refused to have a general strike today, in case workers rallied to the truckers cause and instead called for an evening rally in the centre of Athens. Despite that railway workers were out and so were bus workers during the day.

Wed 29, September 2010 @ 19:04

VN Gelis said…

Despite the death of the trucker, no left protest march occurred as after all he was a worker who has just been made bankrupt and the purpose of the left is to maintain disunity, division and ensuring with all its organised forces that the 'workers disunited will always be defeated'.

All night union meeting occurred in the trucker's headquarters with many rank and file truckers locked out of the headquarters. As there are different sections of the union, and different sub-sections, public service truckers (delivery vehicles) i.e. to hospitals, schools, sewage clearance etc. there are also private sector truckers for supermarket deliveries, retail etc. who controls each section and who takes decisions without informing the base is what the conflict has boiled down to at the moment as the government is threatening to lock them all up and they aren't backing down.

The old leaderships are now in conflict with the Strike Committee who are organised around the various blockades and they want a say if any decision is taken against them. The Minister for Economic (non) Development said he would meet the leaders of the various unions and cut a deal to end the strikes. They voted to end the strikes to restore 'peace in the market' which is collapsing due to the non-delivery of goods from the ports and the evident shortages in a whole range of shops. The leaders of the Strike Committees claimed they weren't consulted again. The anger boiled over when truckers outside the union lit a firecracker against the union sell out leaders.

The leader of the Strike Committee declares here that they will meet on Friday (today) to vote against the sell-out.

http://www.zougla.gr/page.ashx?pid=2&cid=0&aid=177679

A note: some of the union leaders of the 9 Federations which voted to end the strike are members of the Left KKE and Syria (public sector truckers)

Fri 01, October 2010 @ 09:39

Fri 01, October 2010 @ 09:39
Jason said…

Thanks for these updates. Keep them coming.

Sun 03, October 2010 @ 09:31
VN Gelis said…

Ok, Jason.

The 2nd strike appears to have ended, one of the reasons being that the

Strike Committee didn't choose to take control of the situation and expel the old leaderships proposing itself as the way forward. The media made a big hue and cry about the costs to the economy being so far E1.5billion and tonnes of goods trapped in containers in the ports. Immediately after the ending of the strike the Chinese Premier was in Athens giving a speech about how they will buy up Greek bonds and not allow the country to default.

Taking into account Greece is run by the ship-owners this brings to mind a little known deal that was attempted in the late 1960's by the then ship-owners Onassis and Niarhos who wanted to own and control all public facilities, ports, oil refineries, transport under the title Omega Project. If the Chinese want a foothold in Europe and they are using bankrupt Greece as its base this will intensify competition with Germany, who is Europe's biggest export earner?

Next on target are the railways, the solicitors, the chemists as well as the national Electricity company which has just massively increased its rates for all low income earners where liberalisation processes will be rammed through. The Minister of Health Loverdos stated that if we fail in our IMF course, Greeks may resort to a 2nd Goudi, which was the onset of Greek nationalism at the turn of 20th century which started the movement for the re-unification of Greek lands against the decaying Ottoman Empire and the weakening of the European (German) imposed monarchy on Greek political life.

Mon 04, October 2010 @ 09:39
VN Gelis said...

Greek police storm Acropolis protesters today due to protest by unpaid part-time museum workers.

http://www.bbc.co.uk/news/world-europe-11539758

Bus drivers are now under attack facing a 20% wage cut and privatisation.

Train drivers of the national railways as well.

Local elections are scheduled in November where PASOK are expected to get a drubbing with a mass boycott by the electorate. From IMF headquarters in Washington stories are circulating that Papandreou knew the extent of the budget deficit prior to taking power and kept it hidden - a byword to drop him if there is an electoral collapse...

Thu 14, October 2010 @ 23:51
VN Gelis said...

Leaflet: Abstain from Greek Elections!

ABSTAIN!
Don't Participate in these forthcoming elections and give a democratic legalization to the double Papandreic coup

1) In the abolition of the Constitution and the monstrous subjugation of the country to the dictats of the IMF

2) On the servile plan called Kallikratis and the division of the country into 13 self-governing cantons to be easily privatised and added to neighbouring states.

3) Send a message that we no longer expect anything from the collaboration of the parties. They created a storm expect a hurricane in return

www.patari.org

ΑΠΟΧΗ!

ΜΗΝ δίνετε με την συμμετοχή σας σ' αυτές τις εκλογές δημοκρατική νομιμοποίηση στο διπλό παπανδρεϊκό πραξικόπημα.

1) Στην κατάλυση του Συντάγματος και την αυθαίρετη υπαγωγή της χώρας υπό την κηδεμονία του ΔΝΤ.

2) Στο ύπουλο σχέδιο «Καλλικράτης» και την διάσπαση της χώρας σε 13 αυτοκυβερνώμενα καντόνια, εύκολα ιδιωτικοποιήσιμα και προσαρτήσιμα σε γειτονικά κράτη.

ΣΤΕΙΛΤΕ με την Αποχή σας ισχυρό μήνυμα ότι δεν περιμένουμε πλέον τίποτε από την συμπαιγνία των κομμάτων. Έσπειραν ανέμους, θα θερίσουν θύελλες.

www.patari.org   ΚΔΕ-Πατριωτική Αριστερά

Eyewitness Account: Local Elections to Become IMF Plebiscite?

On 7th November Greece goes to the polls under the infamous Kallikratis plan which creates 13 federated regions for the whole country, with one region Attiki (Athens basin) having 50% of the overall population of the country. The Kallikratis plan creates Super-Mayors with powers reminiscent of governors of ancient Rome. In essence they herald the break-up of central government as they aim to merge thousands of local councils and give Presidential powers to each Mayor in each of the 13 regions. Under this background Papandreou announced last night (25th October) if he doesn't win a single region he will resign and go towards new national elections.

Having attacked on behalf of the IMF-EU creditors vast swathes of the population, pensioners, farmers, small shop owners, workers, unemployed whilst not having imprisoned or even attempted to prosecute a single higher ranking government official or MP involved in bribery scandals for public contracts with foreign multinationals (Siemens being one of them). Already according to media reports one in ten are in food kitchens organised around the churches and the constant increases in VAT rates (food to go from 11% to 13% under EU pressure) are constantly eroding the buying power of those in work. Youth of working age from 18-25% who aren't in education or training are more than 80% unemployed supported by families or relatives. The attacks on millions of pensioners with the lowering of pensions has the effect of undermining the social safety net which operates in place of the government. Papandreou realising an electoral wipe-out is on the cards and that he might become the one use Prime minister, attempted to bribe the electorate offering E100 to each pensioner after having cut hundreds already. In addition to this in order to confuse the electorate we have 2 or 3 PASOK prospective candidates in each region with the majority of them declaring they are independent from PASOK without actually having broken from PASOK or even having a single vote in their past which went against the government. Almost all are calling these elections therefore a plebiscite on the IMF.

IMF-Will not avoid social explosion

With daily strikes and struggles all isolated and separate from each other (school students, national railways, part-time museum workers, newsagents etc.) the Left is going from one crisis to the next. Remembering the poor districts of Athens which happen to be in the centre, a leader of the Eurostalinists (who have now split into three factions) Malavazos attempted to speak to an angry public and got yoghurt on his face. The same happened a week before to the KKE's candidate. As for the PASOK and New Democracy candidate they dare not even show their face. Crime, prostitution, unemployment and ghettoization with the constant arrival (100,000 in the first six months of 2010) of destitute illegal immigrants has led to conflict in the central Athenian districts which are starting to resemble 'war zones'. Add to it the daily rise in unemployment there are no jobs, houses, even food so many sleep in abandoned buildings or in town squares. Under the guise of Greece being unable to control its borders the EU is to send an army (NATO) to Evros (region bordering with Turkey) thus complementing the twin role of the IMF-EU occupation. A NATO presence on Greek soil will obviously have one aim and one aim only, to be used against the Greek population in a period of economic and political instability.

So the issues that arise in the current period is that the Left continues to disintegrate and with its influence where one would have assumed they would have proven to be a beacon to the population, it continues its policy of supporting separatist struggles without campaigning for them to unite. It might assume that standing candidates in these sham elections (as all economic and political decisions are now taken jointly by the IMF-EU) and that an increase in their votes, due to the fall of the two main parties may allow them a breathing space, cannot be seen on the ground, as no significant IMF imposed measure has been defeated. Without a single defeat of any IMF-EU measure, the issue that will dominate after the public plebiscite of the IMF in the forthcoming elections, will be whether new elections can forestall the coming social explosion or the expulsion of the IMF occurs as a consequence of these new elections...

Wed 27, October 2010 @ 21:54

There is discussion that if during the first round of local elections this Sunday the ruling party PASOK doesn't achieve a reasonable result they will cancel the 2nd round and go for national elections thus forcing the population to vote for govt thus artificially increasing their capability. A condition for this may be the departure of the PM either after the elections or before.

The sudden appearance of alleged anarchist terrorists once more as in May (though never have any been seen or shown in any media outlet) may serve the purpose of creating more police presence on the streets by creating a climate of fear as bankruptcy is hanging like the sword of Damocles on the Greek electorate if they don't vote as ...advised.

Thu 04, November 2010 @ 22:55
VN Gelis said...

The abstention rate seems to be massive with over half or around just under half voting depending on the 13 Prefecture districts under which these elections are being held. 10% of those that did vote voted white/blank vote (allowed in all Greek elections). So far 5 of the 13 areas are with New Democracy (Right) which implies Papandreou may go for national elections so as to avoid going to a 2nd round of local elections (under the Kallikratis changes) and not gain any large Prefecture.

This abstentions rate is similar to so far to the Euro-election abstention rate.

Left

The KKE has increased its electoral showing so far on a smaller voter turnout but if they don't come 2nd in any Prefecture they don't get through to the 2nd round if it is held.

The Syn/Syriza (ex-Euros) who have had 3 representatives in the Athens area has suffered big defeats.

So far there is a big anti-IMF swing taking into account Greeks generally vote so abstention here appears to be taking the form of an anti-IMF plebiscite and the two main parties have lost significantly from the lack of voter turnout and the swing away from them is big.

So until the elections are finally over (Monday morning) and the main parties make their positions felt we have to wait and see if Papandreou departs as all the media is stating that he does not want to be known as the Prime-Minister who bankrupted Greece (as discussion is occurring constantly about a 'controlled bankruptcy' of Greece) and all the entails:

i) controlled bankruptcy leading to a possible departure from the Euro,

ii) expulsion of the IMF,

iii) possible coalition governments

not of course in that order or all of them at the same time but these are being discussed widely...as possible future scenarios.

Sun 07, November 2010 @ 19:47
VN Gelis said...

A 40-50% abstention rate added with 10% blank/spoiled vote means that both of the two main parties have lost around 50% of their own electoral base. This has been translated by the FT in an article as a vote for the IMF austerity measures, i.e. the bankster's interest paying bond holdings.

http://www.ft.com/cms/s/0/3315f114-ea7c-11df-b28d-

00144feab49a.html?ftcamp=rss#axzz14dBSbhbL

The Right hasn't increased its vote so much as to gain from the electoral fallout of PASOK. If they therefore go for a 2nd round and not for national elections, the Right may gain and PASOK may lose more than 50% of the 13 Prefectures, with a possible increase in abstention as the Left won't vote for the two main parties' candidates in any shape or form.

Sun 07, November 2010 @ 21:37
VN Gelis said…

Papandreou announces he won't go for national elections in the end.

PASOK won 8 out of 13 Prefectures now they have to try to keep them

when they go for the 2nd round. In areas where they gained more than

50% of the votes there will be no 2nd rounds, which so far are 3.

Near enough final results

Abstention, blank and spoiled ballots 45,47%

PASOK: 19,07%

NEW DEMOCRACY: 18,37%

Abstention rate in 2006 last local elections was 37%

The KKE has increased its votes to 14% in the Athens basin

and will get in total around 200,000 votes.

So on the basis of the figures presented

1 in 10 of the official electorate (from which thousands have been added

fraudulently in the last years on the electoral rolls) voted for PASOK.

This is the lowest share of the vote for any party in power since 1975 and it

is only two months since the IMF measures have hit the pay packets of workers and pensioners.

Will the Left campaign now for abstention from the elections

where they can't stand candidates nor will they indirectly call for a vote for the Right to defeat PASOK over the next week? Or will they call for a vote for PASOK to not bring back the Right (section of the Euros may go for this)

Mon 08, November 2010 @ 09:04
VN Gelis said…

On the same day reports are posted about the 'low turnout' in the Burmese elections:

http://www.guardian.co.uk/world/2010/nov/07/burma-election-turnout-low

the extremely low turnout in the Greek elections isn't necessarily headline news.

One wonders why? The day after the next round of elections the IMF arrives again for a new batch of measures. The message being, you voted, you shall pay.

Mon 08, November 2010 @ 17:44
VN Gelis said…

For those who missed it today or didn't catch it an interesting piece on Greece in today's Guardian

http://tinyurl.com/264ace5

Some of the comments are also worth reading and they are many....

Tue 09, November 2010 @ 22:36
VN Gelis said…

Athens Region Final Results

Electors 465.888

Voted: 200.282 / 42,99 %

Valid: 184.241 / 91,99 %

Spoiled: 9.841 / 4,91 %

Blanc: 6.200 / 3,10 %

Abstention, Spoiled, Blank: 60,5%

Just below 4 out of 10 voted in these local elections.

The KKE has called for abstention in the next round.

Wed 10, November 2010 @ 00:03
VN Gelis said…

Abstention as expected reached around 68% in the Athens basin for the Mayors position. Add to it the blank/spoiled ballots and another 12% didn't vote.

PASOK achieved a majority with 11.5% of the voting electorate winning 8 out 13 Prefectures.

This they stated is popular recognition that more IMF measures are required as today they arrive once more in Athens. More will follow once all the results are analysed

Mon 15, November 2010 @ 10:06

Greece: A Tsunami of Strikes amidst continued Disunity on the Left

Despite the recent electoral wipeout of PASOK the government is insistent in implementing every IMF measure turning the country back to the 19th century in terms of labour relations. The new laws have provoked a massive reaction. Having therefore announced they are going to implement the changes to the labour law abolishing collective bargaining, the privatisation of all state owned corporations and continuing indefinitely the IMF payments to foreign bond holders, a tsunami of strikes are occurring this week with a General Strike on 15th December and continued transport strikes as this is being written.

7th General Strike-Union Parades

Following the well-worn pattern of meeting in different squares the Greek TUC with ADEDY (UNITE in Greece) and PAME (KKE's) Union Federation marched towards Parliament and Sindagma Square and the usual union parades didn't take the same course of events as expected. For the last week there have been strikes on different days in the railways, the buses, the banks, air traffic control Aegean Airways etc. A general strike was called, the last of the year, 7th in total, of the by now monthly on average response since the IMF arrived in Greece.

Police Provocation?

The size of the demo once more was impressive. Probably the largest since the large demo on 5th May (which led to the death of 3 bank workers at Marfin Bank) probably between 150-200k and the social composition of the crowd wasn't the usual 'suspects' of the Left, but many working class people with many students and university youth this time, influenced immensely by the struggles that have erupted in Britain, Italy, Portugal and Spain in the last period, showed a persistence of not wanting to leave the streets. The government had thousands of police and riot police present. They even brought the infamous Dias (motorcycle cops). The police sensing the crowd had 'evil' intentions, wanting their salaries and pension cuts reversed and the IMF out of the country, out of nowhere from the ranks of the demonstrators a couple of black clad characters threw Molotov cocktails, smoke and sound bombs to a group of riot police in the front of the Grande Bretagne Hotel on the corner of Sindagma Sq. opposite Parliament. Was this another police provocation to disperse the demo?

What then followed was a violent police reaction with the aim of dispersing the thousands of demonstrators who were on a circular route back towards Omonia and the offices of GSEE passing Parliament on the way. The demo was attacked by teargas and police charges in many different places splitting it into three. The KKE rushed away from the scene of the conflict going towards the other direction of everybody else. Due to the mayhem attacks started to occur to various government buildings such as the Ministry of Economics and the National Post Office as well as the Greek TUC building which was attacked. The police dropped volumes of tear gas making demonstrating near enough impossible.

Ex-Greek Minister of Transport=Early Xmas Present
During the last week a near insurrection has occurred in the area on the outskirts of Athens called Katia after hundreds of riot police are enforcing an EU directive to introduce a new dump site after the previous ones have been labelled full. Daily fines have been imposed on Greece by Brussels numbering in the tens of thousands of Euros. Without asking the local population they have imposed a dump site. Over a period of a year protests have occurred and resistance. On Sunday a real insurrection occurred with the local population arming itself with sticks, stones, even weapons and charging against the hundreds of riot police. Battles occurred overnight with many injured on both sides.

On Monday over 2,000 police, firefighters and navy port workers demonstrated in Athens against the IMF cuts in their wages and benefits which they alleged to be in the region of 20%. Under this background of increased restiveness in many sections of the population when the General Strike came under attack people reacted. They came across an MP and attacked him.

The media which was also on strike didn't report initially anything. It was widely reported on the internet. But the press bureaus of the Left (KKE, Sinaspismos, Democratic Left) condemned the attack. Not a word about what happened in Keratea where many more heads were cracked open. All the parliamentary parties are sensing a social storm is coming. Privatising everything and abolishing collective bargaining will destroy the labour movement in its entirety. This is a battle that cannot be lost. The divisions in the Left have to be overcome and the unions should start to coordinate their strikes indefinitely. Without a political orientation to fight for power, get the IMF out, a social explosion without leadership Argentinian style will provide the alternative, due to the vacuum of the Left. Either which way more incidents against MP's will be on the cards

Euro, Ireland and Usurious Debts

Monstrous

Whilst power is being transferred slowly out of the national terrain into the hands of the unelected EU-IMF vultures, with only a quisling role assigned to the governments of Greece and Ireland (and soon Portugal and Spain), it is becoming clear that the project for a European Union with a single currency but 16 different governments is unravelling right before our eyes. No serious commentator believes it will survive in its present form.

The stage will arrive in the not too distant future, if it isn't actually here already, that the blood required by the vultures of the EU-IMF will no longer be able to be given. Bankruptcy and default of all foreign debts will occur. What does the Weekly Worker assume is going to happen next? That the euro will continue and that the nations of Europe will not fight against their erasure - as announced by Herman Van Rompuy, president of the European Council, in a speech to the EU, when he stated that the nation-states are dead?

Where national sovereignty is threatened, economic decisions are passed to the control of unelected bureaucrats - historically Ireland voted 'NO' in the Lisbon treaty referendum, but then had to vote 'yes' in a rerun. A rebellion starting on national terrain will be the next stage of political developments - the City of London has allegedly made loans to the tune of £150 billion and a default on these debts will mean it takes a hit. This will be a progressive outcome, shifting the balance away from the bloodsucking banksters back to the people.

In attacking the future nationalist response of the Irish people, the Weekly Worker appears to want these monstrous, usurious debts to be paid.

VN Gelis

If only

VN Gelis decries the statement by European Council president Herman Van Rompuy that the "nation-states are dead" (Letters, December 2). As a Marxist, I could only rejoice if such a statement were actually true!

Surely, a basic requirement of internationalism is a view that the nation-state is historically dead, and the progressive solutions we need and fight for can only be achieved over its grave, and on the basis of the development of much wider associations. Previous crises in the European Union have provided the fuel to drive towards much greater integration within it, and it is almost certain that, however much nationalists like VN Gelis dislike the idea; such will be the case this time too.

S/he says that no serious commentator believes that the euro can survive in its current state. That is quite clearly false. Although it's possible that the euro may cease to exist in its present form, and I have explored the possibility of that myself, the reality is that it most likely will continue to exist in its present form, and there are plenty of serious commentators who hold that view. The reality is that the euro is a political project. At the end of the day, the political forces behind that project will do whatever is needed to ensure it continues. In a recent TV interview, Spanish Prime Minister José Luis Rodríguez Zapatero was only the latest leader to spell out what that means: constructing a fiscal union to go along with the monetary union. Already, it has been agreed that next year the EU will issue its own bonds to raise capital in the markets, and that is just another step down the road of constructing a federal European state.

As Marxists, we should welcome such a development, whilst fighting to try to ensure that the basis upon which this new state is constructed is as favourable to workers as we can possibly achieve. But, as a nationalist, VN Gelis cannot think in terms of such an international struggle by workers, because her/his mind is imprisoned within national borders, and as such s/he ends up advocating the preservation of the existing reactionary capitalist states as though that were in some way preferable.

S/he says: "Where national sovereignty is threatened, economic decisions are passed to the control of unelected bureaucrats." But, within the confines of a global capitalist system, the question of national political sovereignty is irrelevant in such matters, especially for tiny economies such as Ireland. The reality is that both Greece and Ireland were already threatened by decisions made by people who were unelected, other than by their shareholders - not people in the International Monetary Fund or in the EU, but by the managers of the huge global bond funds, who refused to buy Irish debt other than at increasingly exorbitant interest rates!

Moreover, while s/he is right to point out that the officials at the European Central Bank and in the EU commission are unelected (although of, course, the finance ministers who ultimately brokered this deal are elected), s/he fails to recognise that the state officials within any capitalist state, including those who run the national central banks, are likewise unelected. Why does s/he think that an unelected Irish bureaucrat determining Irish economic policy is any better than an unelected EU bureaucrat?

The answer here is not to present national capitals or national state bureaucracies as somehow preferable, but to fight for a consistent democracy within the EU itself. In fact, even a consistently bourgeois democratic EU would be better able to withstand the pressure from specific sections of capital than would an Irish workers' state. If we really want to talk about exercising democratic control over economic decision-making, then it is inconceivable that this could be achieved on any basis less than something of the size of the current EU. That is one reason we should welcome its development.

http://boffyblog.blogspot.com/
Arthur Bough

Arab Revolutions harden protestors' resolve in Greece's Eighth General Strike

23 February. On the surface it all looked the same; another day, another general strike, the eighth since the massive 24-hour general strike in May last year which ended with the death of two bank workers. But underneath, the political climate has changed and there is a growing determination to kick-start a more sustained, generalised struggle.

Greece has now had eight general strikes in 10 months, but for the first time demands were raised by a section of the wider political forces of the left to turn Sindagma Square into Tahrir Sq. in Cairo. Moreover, three new elements have been added to the scene: two significant social movements (WE WONT PAY, KERATEA) and the creation of a new political formation SPITHA (Spark).

This latest general strike was as big as the one in May and ended after five hours of battles and tonne's of tear gas being sprayed repeatedly to disperse the crowds. The police deployed their new little toys (noise bombs as well as smoke bombs) where you get the feeling you are in the middle of a war zone as well as the using riot police on motorbikes to ram into demonstrators. Police brutality was pervasive.

Of course, Greek politicians and the media which condemned government violence in the Arab world had no problem supporting the same at home. The irony wasn't lost on the protestors who did everything in their power to liberate any youth that were snatched by police.

The riot police and its special sub-sections the DIAS contingent (they use motorbikes) charged at protestors in the most violent and gangster fashion. Inevitably, one of them couldn't swivel around fast enough and was attacked for trying to ram into crowds and he ended up burning from a Molotov cocktail that was thrown at him.

Arab Revolution

Since the last Greek general strike we have had the significant developments of the Arab world just across the Mediterranean. Greeks have been watching with frustration as their own struggles have led nowhere despite the fact that since December isolated and sectional weekly walkouts by transport workers, various walkouts by pharmacists and also hospital doctors as well as some walkouts by teachers have taken place.

It has become difficult to get to and from work for hundreds of thousands of workers and it is hard for many to get prescription medication due to the IMF-imposed economic "restructuring". Unemployment has hit 15% officially and the economic situation goes from bad to worse. The promised "light at the end of the tunnel" recedes ever further.

Thessaloniki, the country's second city, officially now has 25% unemployment and it is no coincidence that a section of the strikers parked a coffin on Athens' Sindagma Square with a big banner stated 'We Are Dying'. Alongside this the government has announced it has to find €50bn by selling off whatever the country now owns. Finally, they want to cut all social benefits after six months and to abolish all collective wage bargaining and thereby get rid of the 8-hour day and introduce Sunday working.

We Won't Pay

Constant and incessant price rises (20-40%) in public transport has led to a movement which is supported by the wider forces of the left. Numerous non-payment mobilisations have occurred, either during some workday mornings or on Sundays when dealing with motorway tolls. They gather at various stations (bus and metro) and cover all ticket machines and ask for passengers to refuse to pay.

This has met with wide popular support so far and provoked the IMF spokespersons of PASOK in parliament to call those who refuse to pay, "cheapskates" – unlike MPs of course who have no problem accepting bribes for public sector contracts (eg. Siemens) and who, due to parliamentary immunity, have never been prosecuted.

They want to change the laws now and prosecute the 'we won't pay' movement so citizens can be imprisoned or have their assets frozen. This movement has the possibility of gaining a mass following as the crisis deepens and it is showing unity on the ground in struggle by the various forces of the Left. But it still is at its early stage of development.

Keratea

An area on the outskirts on Athens has been chosen by the PASOK government arbitrarily to become a new landfill site as the old ones are now full. Without asking the population or even informing them, they started to stake out the site and move trucks in to do the work.

No one is informed that their area will change and the decisions are imposed from on high. None of these drastic changes ever affect the rich suburbs of north Athens where most of the politicians and businessmen live. As such Greeks have protested on the main highways leading into Keratea and for over two months a police/riot police occupation has occurred with running battles nearly every Sunday, house to house searches and imprisonment of youths with trumped up charges.

But thousands of citizens have refused to yield; they have marched continuously, they have blockaded courthouses to pressurise judges to release their imprisoned friends and they have created a movement which the left has come to support in a limited way, with concerts and solidarity appearances at the militant roadblocks.

Spitha

The citizens' movement around Spitha and the personality of the Greek composer Theodorakis is the newest political development which has been supported by the Lawyers Union, the pharmacists etc. and it attracted a few thousand on the day of the general strike. They ended up at the head of the Greek TUC-ADEDY (public sector union) led march which was literally a few hundred metres behind the KKE-PAME led demo. They marched from the offices of the Greek TUC- Pedion Areos Sq. whilst the KKE started from Omonia Sq. This division has continued now eight times.

Spitha marched under a banner which said: **'No to the Sellout of our Lives and the Sellout of Greece' 'Greece Belongs to the Greeks'** They chanted a variety of slogans: **'Bread Peace Freedom, the Junta didn't Finish in 1973'**

'No to the new junta' The people don't forget they hang traitors'

'Papandreou the people don't want you take the Troika (IMF-EU-ECB) and Go!'

'Cancel all Payments to Foreign Bond Holders'

'National Independence, we owe Nothing to USA Germany'

'Papandreou you will have Mubarak's Fate'

They called on all to occupy the square and they achieved this for many hours but the police were well organised and teargased the area for a long time, thus making it impossible to breathe. Alongside

Spitha, Alavanos who leads one of the three splinter groups of the old Euros also called for Sindagma to become like Tahir, he stayed in the square personally for some time. This is the first time a leader of the Left has asked for this since last May.

Is it sincere or a way of maintaining his own supporters in check? We will see in the next wave of battles.

KKE

Once more the KKE marched quickly and swiftly having a second round of police (its own) in front of the police in Parliament. Citizens who were in Sindagma Square criticised them by being ironic see you on 25th March (which is independence day) for being a Parade, i.e. they march past Parliament, they don't even make speeches there anymore on platforms and they quickly dispersed as if they are leading sheep. Most of their supporters had their heads down when confronted by this tactic which has been inaugurated by the KKE since last May.

Their leader Papariga announced on TV the night before they are expecting provocations and they don't want their contingent attacked and they want to demonstrate peacefully. Parliamentary careerism till the end even when the Greek Parliament no longer dictates economic policy but just implements every new demand from the IMF and the EU.

Despite it appears the recent developments in the Arab world, the majority of the leaders of the Greek Left have learnt nothing and they do not appear to want to change course. If they had called for the people to remain in the square and had campaigned for it previously combined with something more than another 24 hour strike, the passion, courage, determination of the Arabs to fight against all odds would have appeared in an EU country.

It didn't occur this time round, the numbers of people on the ground and the solidarity shown to each by the individual demonstrators against the constant police charges, indicate that the Greeks may have been defeated by the government cuts, but their spirit isn't broken. In the next wave, it's the spirit of the people to march united until the IMF-government programme is defeated.

Mon 28, February 2011 @ 12:13

VN Gelis said...
Committees Against Non-Payment website:
http://www.epitropesdiodiastop.blogspot.com/

Website of militant citizens of Keratea http://lavreotiki.com

Spitha Movement http://www.mikis-theodorakis-kinisi-anexartiton-politon.gr

Main Speech Mikis Theodorakis **http://tinyurl.com/6jp6s9q**

Mon 28, February 2011 @ 19:11
VN Gelis said...

Extensive battles again today in Keratea, police and protestors injured
http://www.zougla.gr/page.ashx?pid=2&aid=270079&cid=4

There have also been protests by a theatre director called Kollatos outside the ex-PASOK Prime Ministers house in the posh district called Kolonaki in the centre as well as outside another PASOK's MP's house former Defence Minister Tzohatzopoulos who has ended up with 76 properties one of which is on one of the most expensive streets in Athens, Areiopaigitou opposite the Acropolis. Around a 1,000 protestors stayed for some time chanting slogans against them. A section of the media has noted that the people are self-organising themselves outside the traditional parties...

Sun 06, March 2011 @ 18:36

Greece: The 'Wall' and Illegal Immigration
Demos Against Illegal Immigration Hit Athens...

A 44year old Greek just about to take his wife to a maternity word in central Athens was killed in the early hours of the morning for his personal belongings. Tonight a demo has occurred and riot police have been called out. Greece was created post-war in the image of America but it never fully industrialised as joining the EU was supposed to lead to that, not turn it into a failed state of Europe, with all that entails.

The Euro project could not work if one had different countries and different policies as credit occurred on a national basis and developed through local knowledge and history based on specific trading conditions and you have different national histories, culture, traditions. Selling Greek products cheaper in Germany than in Greece whose average wages are less than half German ones and when you have imbalances in the welfare state where Greeks do not have welfare payments beyond one year implies that once people run out of money and sell off what they can, starvation hits the door. In Argentina after the growth of the piqueteros movement (this has yet to start in Greece but will emerge by those who don't wish to migrate but stay and fight) the government there introduce a family payment to arrest a situation of dual power developing.

Societies abhor vacuums and this disenfranchisement will force people into action. The Left is slowly starting to realise by pressure from below that this crisis isn't going away as Argentina collapsed by 11% of GDP before a social explosion occurred. We aren't there yet, but well on the way...

VN Gelis

Tue 10, May 2011 @ 23:32

ΕΛΛΗΝΕΣ ΠΟΛΙΤΕΣ ΤΗΣ ΑΘΗΝΑΣ

OXI ΣΤΗΝ ΟΙΚΟΝΟΜΙΚΗ ΕΞΑΘΛΙΩΣΗ ΤΩΝ ΕΛΛΗΝΩΝ
OXI ΣΤΟΝ ΔΙΩΓΜΟ ΤΩΝ ΕΛΛΗΝΩΝ ΑΠΟ ΤΙΣ ΓΕΙΤΟΝΙΕΣ ΤΗΣ ΑΘΗΝΑΣ
OXI ΣΤΑ ΠΑΡΑΝΟΜΑ ΑΦΟΡΟΛΟΓΗΤΑ ΜΑΓΑΖΙΑ ΤΩΝ ΑΛΛΟΔΑΠΩΝ

**Ο ΠΛΟΥΤΟΣ ΤΗΣ ΠΑΤΡΙΔΑΣ ΕΙΝΑΙ ΤΟΥ ΛΑΟΥ
ΕΞΩ ΟΙ ΠΡΟΔΟΤΕΣ ΚΑΙ ΤΟ Δ.Ν.Τ.**

ΑΝΤΙΔΡΑΣΗ ΑΝΤΙΣΤΑΣΗ ΕΞΕΓΕΡΣΗ

ΣΥΓΚΕΝΤΡΩΣΗ-ΣΥΛΛΑΛΗΤΗΡΙΟ-ΔΙΑΜΑΡΤΥΡΙΑ

**ΣΑΒΒΑΤΟ 15.01.2011 ΩΡΑ 12 ΤΟ ΜΕΣΗΜΕΡΙ
ΠΛΑΤΕΙΑ ΑΓΙΟΥ ΠΑΝΤΕΛΕΗΜΟΝΑ**
agiospanteleimonas@gmail.com, 6930 304 442

GREEK CITIZENS OF ATHENS

NO TO THE ECONOMIC IMMISERISATION OF GREEKS
NO TO THE EXPULSION OF GREEKS FROM THE CENTRE OF ATHENS
NO TO THE ILLEGAL TRADING OF SHOPS BY IMMIGRANTS

THE WEALTH OF THE COUNTRY BELONGS TO THE PEOPLE
THROW THE TRAITORS OUT AND THE IMF

REACTION-RESISTANCE-INSURRECTION

Leaflet produced by residents of St Panteleomonas district in central Athens

Battles ensued for hours up to and including riot police throwing tear gas into the main church on the square.
What preceded it was a march by the Soros funded NGO's who were attempting to hold a rally in the main square but were disallowed by the local population. Unable to get through the police tear gassed and tried to disperse the Greeks from the square. They failed abysmally as they refused to leave the square and fought back valiantly against superior forces...

The quisling government of Papandreou announced to much fanfare that Greece was going to build a wall in Evros – border region with Turkey to stop the porous borders which sees Greece receiving hundreds of thousands of illegal immigrants who are then stuck in the country with no visible means of support. This has led in recent years to many conflicts with the indigenous population in many of the central Athenian districts.

Eyewitness Account: Keratea in Struggle Against EU Landfill Regulations

Situated in the middle of a green agricultural belt on the way to historical Lavrio (an area that goes back to ancient times) there has been a battle going on between the few thousand citizens and the dictats of the ruling IMF political party PASOK. Despite the fact that 4.5 m Greeks abstained out of a total electorate of 6m in October's regional and local elections, a battle has been waged since November over the decision to place a landfill right in the middle of an archaeological area and an area of natural beauty. The fate of the IMF government may actually be hanging on a thread. A rural area of Athens has been under constant riot police occupation for over 4 months. Daily battles ensue with riot police, tear gas, smoke bombs and baton charges has been the reality for many in that area. How no one so far has died has actually been a miracle.

Keratea Resistance Festival 8-10th April

Supported by the local mayor and the embattled citizens who have built roadblocks and occupation buildings the intellectual middle classes came to support the citizens with shows, art, poetry, plays, music. More than 50 different participating organisations, with around 35,000 people arriving in the embattled zone came over the three day period. Provisional camp sites were set up, mobile toilets, the traditional souvlaki barbeques and copious amounts of wine, beer and ouzo. The working people of Athens showed their solidarity to the citizens.

Riot police in their tens have been stationed in the area for up to 16 hours a day, attacking citizens, hitting pensioners, arresting young people and generally trying to implement the dictats of the government which without consultation decided where to place a new landfill despite court rulings that they cannot be placed on archaeological sites. But the government that wanted to sell off the Acropolis to pay the foreign banksters has no such reservations. Citizens in Keratea described how the riot police invaded their round the clock blockade at 345am and beat the few citizens up there to a pulp by stating at the same time, 'you will all die' go home.

Due to the success of the resistance festival the citizens of Keratea proceeded to a new wave of struggle by digging up the main roads passing between Keratea and Lavrio with road diggers in the middle of the night. When the riot police found out about it the next day they stormed the citizens reaching right up to their houses with many injured on both sides and many going to hospital. No media outlet has gone to interview ANY citizens about the events. It is becoming clear, that without a resolution of this issue the government's dictats are being questioned fundamentally. That implies that either they have to win, or fall

The Left refuses to campaign for the departure of PASOK

Officially only two leaders of the Left (Alavanos-Euros and Theodorakis-Spitha) have gone to Keratea, the KKE has abstained despite its paper support of their struggle in their paper Rizospastis (Radical) and a large mobilisation of the supporters of the left, hasn't been called for. Instead evening style protests where you only hear speeches are made in different Athens squares by different union federations on different days and different times.

Official website of the citizens of Keratea
http://lavreotiki.com/
VN Gelis

Eyewitness Account: Greece One Year of the IMF: Decay and Depression

Economic and Social Crisis

On the anniversary of the IMF-ECB takeover of Greece it would be good to make an assessment of the situation to see what has happened and how the situation might develop in the coming period.

In 2009 the debt was E300 billion and it became E330billion or 140% of GDP and by the end of 2011 it will equal around E350billion or around 150% of GDP. So two years of monetary austerity and widespread cuts in pensions, wages, etc. has led to an increase in the debt and a massive increase in the percentage of debt in relation to GDP. The government has stated that public debt will drop to 60% of GDP within a decade and one would require an average growth rate of 6.5%. That isn't occurring as in 2010 the actual economy declined by 6%. In 2011 it has been predicted to fall by 4.4%. Son in two years it will decline by 10% of GDP. So depression economics actually increased both debts and deficits and points to only one direction: restructuring of the debt or bankruptcy. Restructuring the debt is a form of bankruptcy as the creditors have to accept a haircut either in the interest rates they expect in return or in the actual amount they have allegedly loaned by buying up government bonds. At the same time due to the overheating of the German economy (rise in exports and inflationary pressures) the ECB has stated that interest rates have to rise. So specifically for the PIGS, when their economy have negative growth rates by increasing the interest rates you push them further into a debt/bankruptcy spiral and push the Euro further onto the path of disintegration. The issue of credit default swaps as well indicates that a section of foreign bankers want bankruptcy to gain from the bets they have made, on the economy tanking.

According now to other figures, Greek social security (IKA) has had a drop in payments from E2.2billion in 2009 to E1.6billion due to the massive rise in unemployment which hovers around 1,000 citizens a month, or 15.1%. Taking into account one is only paid for one full year then when one comes off the unemployment register that does not mean one is now ...employed. Around 800,000 people have lost their work as shop owners and their insurance known as TEVE does not pay any unemployment pay and if you owe more than E8, 000 you cannot claim a pension until you have paid it off. Alongside that they have extended the pensionable age, so if someone is around 55 and his shop has gone bankrupt recently they would not be able to claim a pension or have any health cover for at least 5 years when they are pensioned off, as Greece has a US style health cover system, with payments mandatory on a monthly basis before any cover is granted.

The National Bank of Greece in a recent study stated that average losses for workers in the public sector are equal to 13.5% for the private sector are 14% and for the pensioners around 11.5%. With unofficial inflation running around 7% that equals on average a collapse in average spending power around 20% in one year. This by itself is crippling the private sector as without spending power the market starts to implode as it is doing daily as on average 1,000 are becoming unemployed. The IMF government assumes the whole issue is about public expenditure and the main focus of all government and media propaganda is regarding the high costs of the crippled Greek welfare state.

At the same time we are witnessing the mass de-industrialisation of Greece and the collapse of its agricultural sector whereby for example sugar imports now come from abroad alongside garlic all the way from China, unheard of imports three decades ago when Greece joined the EU under the guise that these sectors would be developed, but instead were destroyed.

The usurious interest rates by the EU are also an amazing feat of modern economics as the ECB loans with 1% interest rates but the pay out of Greek bonds are 6%, thus allowing a difference of 5% which when calculated on a yearly basis is equal for what has been borrowed to E5billion equivalent to the annual wage budget of the public sector. The one which has been targeted to be cut to the bone, privatised, sub-contracted, deregulated and whatever other modern form of slavery collapsing capitalism comes up with.

The level of decay has reached US proportions with the police announcing that women shouldn't travel at night anymore in Athens as they are liable to be robbed and daily we hear stories of bank lootings, supermarket robberies and robberies of pensioners in their homes, unheard of events in Greece. Three four star hotels have closed in the centre of Athens as well which were the pride and joy when the Olympic (Coca Cola) Games hit the town, as well as the recent bloody looting of the Lawyers Union offices in central Athens. But the police has been unable to fill up its cars and no longer turn up for crimes as they cannot/do not want to as even a few of them have fallen victim to shootings.

Media reports also speak about Greeks handing over young children to orphanages for the first time in decades trying to ensure a better life for them. Child benefits are under attack as the latest story is the social security benefits have collapsed due to the ageing population alongside the support provided to neighbouring Balkan states whereby their social security contributions could be added onto the Greek system if they worked in Greece for two years and were near pensionable age. Tens of young women mostly from African countries now ply their trade in central Athenian squares when the sun goes down for as little as 5Euros and there have even been shootouts between indigenous gypsies and Asian beggars in rubbish dumps with a few victims

IMF-ECB 'Troika' vs. Welfare State
A massive programme of cuts in both schools and hospitals has been inaugurated recently by the IMF-ECB. 10% of schools are to be merged, what happens to the positions of staff is still not well explained but a new law is being implemented whereby staff can be made flexible and transferable across the whole of the public sector, including other cities, but if one is already married and they have commitments in one city, this will be an explosive issue alongside the fact that many parents who lived in villages can no longer travel 25km twice daily to take their children to schools. Thus for the first time since the civil war era many will no longer send their children to school. In almost every town square in Athens there are banners up by people announcing their opposition to these mergers. In one town in northern Greece students started a hunger strike in the town square with tents. The IMF-ECB targets primarily the welfare state as they are considered to be unproductive.

Hospital suppliers in medicine have had their payments frozen and they have gone on strike refusing to supply the hospitals. Twice in the last year there has been a non-payments strike and many thousands of Greek citizens relying on medicine have had their supplies cut and have tried to source medicine from abroad to survive. The IMF-ECB has obviously seen how much is being spent on health in general and they have cut the overall budget alongside the fact that they have sub-contracted many essential parts of health care to private companies such as scanning, etc. nutrition. There are 140 govt hospitals and 2 university hospitals. There is talk of merging around 40 of them and over the last two weeks two central university teaching hospitals closed overnight with issues for patients in their care who were advised just to up sticks and leave. Alongside this situation many A&E wards just close down in order to make savings without it being pre-announced. Just before Easter two university hospitals closed down overnight and hospital patients were carted off. The IMF induced measures aim to cripple health and weaken the standards one has been used to accept and return once more to a fully privatised health service, but this has been difficult to openly announce as PASOK is the party that created the Greek style NHS in the 1980's.

Mass privatisation and strikes against the IMF
The government's announcement of the mass privatisation of almost every remaining state interest in transport, energy, land etc. in order to raise E50billion Euros between 2012-2015 aims to destroy all working class gains and reduce the Greek working class into total and absolute penury replacing it as has already occurred in the private sector into a multi-national globalised footloose force which will have no roots, no unions and zero political representation. Under these conditions since the last big general strike various battles have occurred.

In the last 12 months there have been 8 general strikes and two solid truckers' strikes one of which lasted almost one month and was sold out by its union misleaders. There have also been many strikes in the ports which have had only 24 hour duration.

Constant small, but significant battles have occurred by groups of workers in transport, bus and metro and by part-time council workers who have renewable contracts. Bus workers have been the most militant as they have a significant history being the only group of workers who brought down a government in the early 1990's when a previous government tried to privatise them. They have had many mass meetings and have had many days of strike. But the government has been restrained from announcing that they be privatised as the bitter experience of that battle may trigger an indefinite walkout which may become a pole of attraction for other groups of workers. The union tops are obviously trying to let off steam and may end weakening their morale when everyone knows what is needed is joint indefinite strike action by all transport workers or uniting with the movement Can't Pay Won't Pay and calling for workers to travel for free.

Part-time council workers occupied the Athens Mayoral office for the best part of two months demanding full time contracts as some have done the same job for years but have been on part-time contracts so they lose out on other benefits. In the meantime a lawsuit went through the Greek high courts vindicating all part-time workers prior to 2001. This led to the part-time council workers mistakenly ending their occupation.

When the Health Minister Loverdos went to give a speech to an old peoples social centre in a working class district in North Athens Ag. Anargirous he was confronted by pensioners and unemployed youth and this became a national issue for the government as they cannot speak publically almost anywhere anymore without the presence of riot police and tear gas. They have lost almost total support.

Apart from token one day strikes the national rail workers who founded much of the early socialist tradition in Greece at the turn of the last century, there hasn't been any dynamic action when at the same time due to the cuts, all international connections between Greece and the rest of Europe has been cut. No train services now go to Europe at all and taking into account in the summer months many neighbouring countries use them to go on holiday in northern Greece this is a massive collapse of transport relations. Alongside the almost total shutdown of Olympic Airways (despite the electoral announcements by Papandreou that he would support them) and the sell-off of its most profitable routes to the USA, Australia, S Africa where significant Greek communities live abroad, transport in Greece is heading into a transport meltdown for the crucial summer season which brings in tourist revenue.

Joining the Imperialist Armada against Libya

Greece despite its financial situation has had not one iota of apprehension in joining the imperialist armada against Libya with a frigate and the use of all Greek airspace as well as full rights for the US airbase in Suda in Crete. Recently they also held joint military exercises with Israel taking on the role of its best friend at the moment its relations with Turkey have cooled down.

'Can't Pay Won't Pay'-Social Movements

A movement based on not paying road tolls to the large private corporations which got government subsidies to build motorways has been centred on the main national roads and on roads which haven't as yet been built and the cost of driving your car through them took on a national focus. This movement then spread to the metro, tram and bus system in Athens. Price rises of 40% in the last two months on public transport were the issue that provoked this anger giving growth to this movement. We have also had protestors raiding police stations and trying to cancel all the police prosecutions for those who have refused to pay. This is the single issue that has united all wings of the Left. It doesn't have as yet practical public support as people who are working, still have to get to work and one cannot avoid paying tickets all the time, but when the protestors arrive and block the entrance ticket stamping machines, people cannot physically use tickets that they bought. Recently, it is alleged, the machines which issue tickets in one station have been smashed literally by using large hammers.

The PASOK government initially labelled all the protestors 'cheapskates' then as the movement grew into weekly events then daily events in various stations around Athens, they changed tone and started talking about reducing the road tolls by almost 50%. They have announced this to occur, but it hasn't occurred as yet. No movement on reducing the price rises in other modes of transport has been announced.

Meltdown of the Left

The KKE recently held an evening rally which only a few months before would have had a minimum of 15,000 but now only had a couple of thousand and they couldn't even block the roads around Sintagma Square. Soon their evening rallies may be held just on pavements. They offer no fighting programme for the unemployed, they have organised no right to work rallies, they do not campaign for anything more than what the Greek GSEE – TUC does which is 24hour token strikes, the next being 11th May (9th so far) and they continue to march separately, along different routes and disperse in an unheard of destination for all Greek demos, near the tourist area of the Acropolis, avoiding Parliament-Sindagma Sq. in case protestors are emboldened as they were last May to storm it.

The May Day Demo this year had very few participants and it had three different demos, one for the KKE-PAME the other for the Greek TUC-Euros and another for the leftists/anarchists. The KKE's block only had a few thousand and it marched to the French Embassy for the war in Libya. The disunity continues in stark contrast to the battle of Keratea which had zero influence from the Left and stood on its own and forced the government into retreat.

Euros

In a recent meeting on the issue of the Euro and the Debt where representatives of the pro-European wing of the Euros invited S Kouvelakis (from a London University who is allied with C Lapavitsas) to speak who argued that Greece should stop all payments to its creditors, withdraw from the Euro and restore the Drachma as a means of restoring monetary and fiscal policy and introducing controls in the economy as it is faced with a depression and ECB set interest rates which will cripple it further, he was rounded on as wanting to isolate Greece and become a modern version of Albania cut off from the outside world. Kouvelakis avoided calling for the departure of Greece from the EU as this would have been step too far for the Euros and one of their leaders, Lafazanis did ask the audience what would they do if they suddenly found themselves in power? He answered his own question by stating they would be obliged to propose cuts, meaning that once the electoral tap of state funds propping up the official Left runs dry, they may have to repeat 1989 once more (when they last joined coalition governments of both the Right and PASOK). The discussion was centred on managing capitalism as opposed to overthrowing it.

Spitha Movement-Theodorakis

On the other hand there have been many high profile resignations from the Spitha movement due to the backdoor deals between Theodorakis and certain foreign centres of power which seek to promote a government of 'personalities' as opposed to a government of politicians who are so visibly detested in this present juncture, that it appears they are trying to repeat the 'liberalisation' period of the last days of the Greek military junta when a

General called Markezini was propelled to power, but they couldn.t avoid the occupation of the Polytechnic and the subsequent continuous demonstrations which led to the fall of the military in 1974. After the fall, Theodorakis having travelled to the US Pentagon proposed the option of 'Karamanlis or Tanks' with Karamanlis being a Presidential candidate from the Right, in order to block the possibility of a socialist solution to the fall of the junta. As if to underscore this tragedy the name of Markezini has popped up again, but not in the form of the father but the son, who is now a Sir and lives in London as a new interim Prime Minister in the post-Papandreou era, to continue to implement IMF policies, in other words buying time for the oligarchic ruling elites from workers anger. This has created many splits and divisions in this new found movement and it appears Theodorakis was only interested in using those that joined, to a pre-planned hidden agenda.

Committee Against 'Odious Debt'
A group of academics and people from the wider Left has set up a campaign to classify the debt Greece owes to international bankers as being odious and that they should default like the 30odd other countries that have done since the 1970's around the world. The media has presented some of their findings and some of the information regarding their investigations has reached the light of day, like some facts regarding Siemens bribery deals to secure big Greek public defence orders or infrastructure projects as well as the fact that a large percentage of overseas debt is just interest and that the original amounts borrowed have been paid many times over.

Post-Papandreou Era and Continuing the Same IMF Policies...
The PASOK government is a busted flush. Its writ no longer runs as evidenced in Keratea. It has lost almost all credibility. The massive abstention in the local elections when 4.5million Greeks around 85% if the electorate refused to take part in October's 2010 elections indicates a massive swing against all politicians and parties. There are open rebellions in almost every layer of society. They are left with two options. Either to go for new elections or to suspend due process and go for a government of 'personalities' as has been stated has been offered to the Theodorakis movement of Spitha (which was set up officially to be a new force on the Left, not an old one which will collaborate with the IMF!)
The media which in Greece operates as a precursor to events by moulding 'public opinion' has been promoting all the close collaborators of the Spitha movement and all intellectuals both in constitutional affairs also in economics regarding the foreign debt and the agreements with the IMF, showing that they are both unconstitutional and odious and that they should be cancelled forthwith. Whether they are able to postpone the inevitable of Arab style continuous protests in central city squares when unemployment continues to rise inexorably and businesses go bust daily

will be one of the modern wonders of our time. A spark will this time light a fire.
VNGelis

Spitha Movement which became a Personality Cult around Mikis Theodorakis, split and degenerated

May-June Events 2011
The Rise of the Indignants (Aganaktismenoi)

Editor's Note: As was noted in the previous articles Greeks eventually would hit the streets en masse and they did in their millions throughout May-June. This was probably the last peaceful attempt at derailing the IMF and the 300 quisling politicians that prop it up. Left leaderless from now on the script will be written on the street in ways which will encompass past history and current reality.

Greeks Occupy Central City Squares Arab Style

Maria Damanaki ex-KKE but PASOK for the last two decades and a Euro Commissioner http://ec.europa.eu/commission_2010-2014/damanaki/index_en.htm stated in the EU today that 'either the Greeks adopt the 2nd round of cuts and privatisations' with a unity across the two major parties, or Greece will return to the Drachma.

Taking into account her current position as an EU Fisheries Minister, she cannot be saying things without high level agreement with Papandreou. It is being used to threaten and cajole the Opposition Parties (bar the KKE) to allow PASOK to get through its legislative programme of more cuts by forcing the 180 votes required in

Parliament
this time (2/3 of total) otherwise the government will fall. New
Democracy traditionally the pro-American party may be seeking a
Euro exit for Greece.

The government doesn't seek elections as it would lose so it is now
pushing for a Plebiscite for the new round of measures sought by the
IMF

At the same time over the last few days, influenced by the Spanish
events 300 Greeks have occupied Sindagma Square (most of them are ex-
Spitha members) and today they called a Facebook protest on the square
and 150,000 have signed up on Facebook which has collapsed in Greece.

We Have Woken Up- in Both Greek and Spanish

Athens Madrid Lisbon All of Europe on the Path of Struggle are two of
the banners and slogans shouted.

Tell the Government we won't sell our Country; tell the Politicians to
Leave said one demonstrator on live streaming
http://www.zougla.gr/page.ashx?pid=85&playerType=flashe streaming

VN Gelis

All night discussions occurring in the central squares about what to do
next.
A main issue is to stay there until the government leaves or for workers to
join protests nightly after work if they can't be there round the clock.

The discussions are occurring in a fraternal manner and it is reminiscent of
the last days of the junta. The police so far haven't attacked the
demonstrators with tear gas, but the night is long and one doesn't know
what will happen. Some will obviously leave but some will return. The spirit
is to fight, most of the mass media has ignored it, but it is widespread on
the internet.

Facebook and mobile phones where initially blocked in the square but they
have returned. The other issue is whether the organised left will join the
protests and try to derail them into a safe for capitalism direction. There is
a very large component of youth who were organised via the social media
and if it lasts during the night and into the morning it will be difficult to get
Athens moving.

So workers may end up joining the protests in the morning...

Some pictures from Indymedia
http://athens.indymedia.org/front.php3?lang=el&article_id=1295118

26th may-Update
The police didn't tear gas the massed crowds. A contingent of workers
from the electricity workers union GENOP-DEI arrived with a large banner
and the crowd supported them.

They placed their banner and shouted slogans outside the Economics
Ministry which is on Sindagma Sq. which stated We Don't Sell, We Can't
Be Sold and shouted slogans, cheap electricity for the masses.

The main media hasn't really promoted it and Facebook was downed a few
times alongside mobile phone networks in the centre when people were
gathering. The fact that it occurred in every Greek city means there is a
shift now and one doesn't know how it will develop as they aren't controlled
by the trade union bureaucracy or the political Left and as such it is still
new. If nightly gatherings persist and gain in volume it may develop into a
real conflict if it isn't derailed or controlled. But by creating a power
vacuum, with the state not initially intervening in a heavy hand manner
which it has done over the last 12 months every time Greeks have
gathered in the centre, may imply the government is looking for an exit, but
as yet does not know how or where to go...

Slogans from last night:

-EE Oh Oh, take the IMF and Get Out...

-Democracy, Freedom and Justice

-A magical night as in Argentina we will wait to see who gets in the
Helicopters first'

-Greece of Greek bankers, snitches, usurers, exploiters

-'Bread, Education, Freedom, the Junta didn't Die in '73'

-Leave Your Weapons and Join Us

26th May 2011
Although a Greek website one gets a flavour of the demos in the various
cities of Greece including the island Rhodes.

http://www.zougla.gr/page.ashx?pid=2&aid=317762&cid=4

For a second night thousands turned up in Sindagma Sq. and an open air debate occurred. But it started raining...

Some of the slogans that have been heard by the alleged 'apolitical' audience as reported now by the mass media... most of these rhyme in Greek so translation is difficult.

George (Papandreou) you Wanker we Didn't Come Here for a Joke

31st May 2011

The occupation continues for a 7th night.

Some scenes with the background music of a new song by a popular Greek singer called Cooking Pot about how empty it will become.... and a lot more… http://tinyurl.com/6fy4ewf
The media hasn't interviewed people on the square and just mentions it.

7,000 attended a meeting in the centre with Theodorakis as speaker and many shouted for Papandreou to leave now. Theodorakis said this film has been replayed before in 1944 with his grandfather in the same place (implying that this led to defeat of the Left) and he got booed for it...
A video of the speech today. http://tinyurl.com/64ljlc4

From the video one can clearly discern the waving of Greek flags and the social composition of the audience which clearly isn't middle class.Greece will allegedly receive its 5th interim loan this week after agreement by Merkel, but massive cuts in benefits are going to be the payback, so it looks like the demos on the streets of the major cities in Greece will continue as the crisis isn't going away.

1st June
Last night after the Theodorakis speech thousands surrounded the entrances to Parliament changing Thieves Thieves Politicians not allowing them to leave. When some got into their chauffeur driven cars, they were sworn at, rude hand gestures Greek style were made to them and some were followed by old ladies along the narrow pavements. As the police deemed it would spiral out of control some were rushed to other exits than the main ones along dark pathways

leading to the national park adjacent to Parliament.

For the whole of today the mass media has attacked the protestors as being basically hooligans alleging Greeks are as bad as Mugabe and that this is a massive attack on Parliamentarism, not the IMF measures which are crippling the country. They are also alleging that these are acts against democracy and elected Parliament, whilst thieving pensions and creating mass unemployment are obviously democratic acts of a flourishing social system which condemns people to a slow and arduous death. They then brought out the riot police to surround the side entrances to Parliament without attacking the protestors but guarding those who wanted to leave Parliament.

One of the leaders of the Euros today Alavanos, not having appeared to support the movement of the Disgruntled (which is what it is being labelled by the media) stated the Left should depart from Parliament. The peaceful nature of the protests which have gone on for one week now is nearing an end. The situation will end up spiralling out of control. If people in such large numbers have gone on the streets they will end up staying until the govt departs. Already a big banner has replaced all others stating We Will Stay Until the IMF, the Govt and the Debt Goes.

Either the government will have to attack the demonstrators at some stage, or clear the area on some hygiene issue or it will have to depart. What happened last night has raised the morale of all undoubtedly; the streets will undo what the IMF politicians created...

June 3rd 2011

Two events yesterday have hit the mass media.
Govt spokesperson Petalotis went to give a speech at a pensioners club in Argiroupoli a working class district of Athens and the local residents confronted him and he had to be scurried out via the back door.Riot police were called out to control the crowds of workers and pensioners...

In the meantime in Corfu Greek politicians and invited Euro MP's were scurried out by yachts after leaving a hall they were meeting in by a port due to the massed citizens protesting and calling in one of their slogans for the whole of Greece to become like Keratea (are that defeated the IMF govt after they attempted to impose a rubbish dump)

16 PASOK MP's have written a letter to Papandreou showing reservations against the new round of cuts for the 5th interim bailout package which in reality is an accounting trick as no money ever arrives in Greece from the IMF it is just funnelled away from peoples' pockets to the banksters.

The next few weeks are going to be crucial as Greeks are still congregating in the main squares and this Sunday's event is billed to be the biggest ever...

KKE
CP leader Papariga has come out firmly against a return to the drachma and does not even call for elections or the government to go now. It hasn't called its members to take part in the demos in the main squares and it is doing everything in its power to prop up the IMF govt, but it will start to lose many of its younger followers in the coming period...

VNGelis

Eyewitness Account of 5th June protests in Athens occupied Sindagma Square

For more than 11 days Greeks have occupied the main squares in many cities: Athens, Thessaloniki, Patras, Iraklion among them. Left leaderless by all parliamentary parties and under siege from more IMF-imposed measures to save a moribund capitalism, the people are taking matters into their own hands. The wholesale privatisation of Greece is on the cards, prefiguring mass redundancies in the public sector as the Greek Economics Ministry is being directed more and more from Brussels and New York.

A large number of Greeks have decided to camp in the main Athens square opposite Parliament and demand a plebiscite on the EU/IMF-imposed measures. Most of them were organised previously in the Spitha movement associated with Mikis Theodorakis but they became disillusioned with it when they heard there were moves afoot to form a government.

Since then a tidal wave has grown beyond their initial expectations. Many via Facebook started to campaign independently for direct action by occupying squares and when on the evening of 25 May more than 100,000 turned up a new movement was born.

The media has presented the demos as those of the 'Indignant' who aren't political; what they mean is there is no politics because no political party owns it. But in reality the event is deeply political as can be readily seen in the extremely militant slogans, displays and discussions. No one wants anything to be sold, or privatized anymore, or the country to be broken apart and sold off bit by bit to foreign banks.

What we are witnessing are the people in motion against the Parliamentary parties. If there was a real Left it would have quit Parliament and campaigned with the people for an indefinite general strike until the government is toppled, but this clearly does not yet exist.

Throughout the last week more than 500,000 have turned up at Sindagma to show their opposition to the MPs in Parliament. There are essentially four parts to the events that occur:

• **A group of drummers arrive with loudhailers and chant slogans between 7-10pm every evening**

• **The group of 300 hundred occupies the square on the corner and demand a Referendum on the IMF measures**

• **A group that has occupied the main square outside the main metro station hold nightly debates in a Popular Assembly.**

• **There are also groups of artists, intellectuals, poets etc. camped out in the square.**

On Sunday, 5 June, as the sun was going down, massed crowds started to arrive. Pensioners, mothers with their children, disabled wheelchairs users, young people of all ages – all participated in the various events in the centre.

Those who wanted to chant slogans assembled under the two main banners: one read 'Bread Education Freedom, the Junta Didn't Die in 1973 in this square the IMF will fall' and another massive banner carried the slogan 'Out! with a massive picture of a helicopter.

Many crowded the square to engage in political discussions at the various stalls and displays. So many arrived from all over Greece that the police started to use roadblocks in the Corinth area and also they used teargas to block protestors trying to join in the Athens demo at the Evangelismos Hospital.

The Communist Party was on the periphery of yesterday's events, handing out a four colour leaflet advertising all the new measures that the IMF is going to impose – as if the protestors don't know what is coming or aren't fighting against it with their countless original slogans which change daily and are reported by all Greeks to their friends, workmates when they go back home.

In conversation a KKE militant said that even if the IMF is rejected, as it was in Argentina in 2002, nothing will change. The same people condemned their own members this time last year for trying to occupy Parliament, calling them 'provocateurs' and their leader stated openly that she does not condone the disruption of a meeting held by PASOK. Yet she hasn't got a problem when politicians use riot police against peaceful citizens' protests, as everyone knows that they cannot appear in public anywhere anymore without meeting with confrontations and protests.

These daily protests are taking a logic of their own and they will lead inevitably to some form of conflict as the state cannot allow indefinitely for this to go on. They are waiting for it to dissipate. But it has grown stronger up to now. The possibility always exists for a Latin American-style provocation (use of agent-provocateurs amongst the protestors, or use of bombs) and then us this as an excuse to clear the centre, but this will be difficult to sell due to the volume of people participating.

The social crisis is not going on holiday so the situation does not appear to be orientating towards a de-escalation, thought nothing can be totally guaranteed. What is clear is that large bodies of people are now in a political vacuum. No one wants any of the old parties and they openly rally against them. We are clearly in a transitional period where the old is dying and the new has yet to be born.

Mon 06, June 2011 @ 12:43

VN Gelis said...

On Monday the media apart from the govt one was on 'strike' so no reports occurred regarding the size of Sunday's demo. The tickets on the Athens metro were reported to be around 250,000 and only a third ever pay and schools as yet haven't gone on holiday. Last night a Govt Minister went to give a speech in an area of Athens and the police used tear gas for the first time against citizens protesting and they had to get her out on a police motorbike wearing a police helmet.

As far as one can make out the politicians won't be able to travel at all anywhere. The KKE condemned most of these events as a sign of populism and they condemn all signs of violence whatever that implies, as the violence of unemployment, price rises and the IMF of course are 'hidden' from view. As the situation spirals out of control the KKE makes declarations of legality to the state.

Late last night frictions were created in the square as the people who organise the speeches under an umbrella organisation called realdemocracy.gr organised by the Euros who for years carried

Greek flags are now opposed essentially to people who wear flags on their backs and support the demonstrations chanting Hellas Hellas (Greece Greece) alongside other anti-govt slogans. The topic of debate was the issue of the Debt by the 'specialists' those who allegedly are up to the job of analysing the crisis, as if it isn't specialists who already in power...

Tue 07, June 2011 @ 17:26

VN Gelis said...

9th June

General Strike called today by government public services, Post Office plus Savings, Telecoms, Water, Ports, Greek Defence Industry plus Banks. Whistles and hats were distributed by many of the unions and the demos were separate once more but were on the same path. The KKE had around 1,000 whilst the others were at least 5-6 times bigger. The slogans weren't that militant and are clearly behind what is going on Sindagma Sq. They marched passed the Sq. and did not stay there to give speeches, but the midday sun was so hot everybody would have collapsed anyway if it occurred in front of Parliament but it could have occurred at the bottom end of the Square below and it didn't. The union bureaucracy's don't want to be associated with the 'riff raff' on the square presumably.

There are severe difficulties for the govt at the moment as it is being pressurised by the EU-ECB to propose a new round of measures which are agreed by the two main parties PASOK-NEW DEMOCRACY to be sold to the Greek people, but agreement appears to be difficult for it would imply hara-kiri for both.

The issue is now when the vote is alleged to occur on 15th June whether agreement will have been reached by then or whether the govt will have fallen. Another possibility is for a provocation to occur on the square and force the people to go home and they don't appear to be doing so. Each day doesn't have as many but various events increase or decrease numbers accordingly. Many should come again this weekend and if they continue this will put even more pressure on the govt to take some form of action. This situation cannot go on indefinitely and already sections of the media are stating Athens in under siege. Over the last 5-6 general strikes black hooded characters have thrown Molotov cocktails at police ranks right in the middle of the workers demonstrations and then given the green light for the police to attack and disperse the crowds. So far they haven't appeared on the square, but this being Greece, one is sure they are never far away.

Schools are supposed to break up this week and hopefully school students will join the ranks giving new blood to the movement. Greece isn't necessarily like Spain, where it was stated today the camps in the square were withdrawn and it is closer to Egypt. So far it's been peaceful, but for how long especially now that the govt cannot essentially go anywhere. A protest has been designated outside Papandreou's house next Wednesday as well....

Thu 09, June 2011 @ 19:47

VN Gelis said...

11th June

The fallout from the largest ever post-junta rally (mass media now mentions that up to 2 million Greeks may have participated in all the nations squares) has meant that the govt has now announced that the 2nd round of IMF cuts targeting all and sundry from wage cuts to pension cuts, which was to occur on 15th June has now postponed the decision till 28th June, when it was allegedly to occur next week. They are aiming in dragging out the guerrilla war with the protestors up until they give up and go home.

Papariga the leader of the KKE (Communist Party) stated last night that we aren't against the 300 MP's in Parliament as our ones contribute their salaries to their party, as if the issue is solely about what individual MP's do, not the system in place which has allowed Parliament to be a rubber stamping IMF institution. Instead of the Left leaving Parliament and campaigning on the streets, they are embedded to parliamentary 'democracy' till the end. 2 million people have left the traditional parties and aren't going back in this lifetime, so when they chant 'they must all go' the mass media attack them for not offering an alternative, as if one has to offer something first before making demands on the IMF. First the masses have to join the KKE before they can demand PASOK leave, in other words PASOK should stay as the masses haven't joined... the KKE.

Workers, unemployed and pensioners continue to go to the square daily. Sunday is expected to see large numbers again.

Sun 12, June 2011 @ 08:51

VN Gelis said...

14th June

Mass Media calls for Greek Aganaktizmenous-Indignated to Encircle Parliament at 7am

The same call has appeared by those who support the alleged Popular Assemblies in the square at the bottom end of the Square – Euros and other assorted globalists. Up until yesterday i.e. for the whole of the past year, when thousands attempted to do just that they never called for the government to go. They are also calling for all the popular assemblies in every local areas of Athens to have marches and go to Sindagma. The joke with the KKE doing the rounds is that whilst Aleka Papariga its General Secretary for the last decade has called for people to go on the streets and fight, her latest call was for them to go back to the factories and fight the bosses there...

So what could be the purpose of this call by the mass media for people to encircle Parliament? To truly support the populist demands that those who are 'thieves of public money' should be court-martialled like in Goudi or that people should occupy Parliament so the troika of the IMF-EU-ECB are sent packing?

Impossible when taking into account that the Greek media networks are owned by the biggest capitalist sharks that own or take most of the public sector contracts when they come up and are those who are the best lackeys of the IMF-EU. What is being played therefore? But as with every protest movement capitalism seeks to subvert it, utilise it for its own ends and move on, without uprooting the fundamentals. It's no coincidence that for 3 weeks the media has been absent from the square as after all the protestors have chanted 'Scumbags, Grassers, Journalists' and have chanted against two journalists from Mega TV (which has supported the IMF continuously beyond what is necessary even by their own terms) one being female calling her 'Olga Tremi Paid Whore' and Prenteri the Overturn of the System aren't a Media Show'. The latter threatened the protestors in an article in the main national daily Ta Nea with a provocation on the square stating that these types of protests occurred in the mid-19th century in France and when somewhere shot, causing havoc, the army came out to 'restore order' so they should watch what they wish for as the ...worst could develop.

There could be a possibility for provocation Marfin (when bank workers were burnt to death allegedly by anarchist provocateurs but most probably by the security services) style. There could also be the possibility that this government will fall and a new government of 'technocrats' and 'personalities' takes over to try and continue the

IMF dictats but this time by 'popular will' i.e. the pressure of events on the streets. Tomorrow will show.

There will be a widespread general strike tomorrow and for the first time the union federations (GSEE-TUC and KKE-PAME) will march under the background of protests which have already occurred encompassing the overwhelming majority of Greeks who have been in squares for approximately 3 weeks. Many of their members have been on the demos on their own. So will they march together or separately? Will they stay in the squares and encourage the encirclement of Parliament? Will the riot police attack to disperse the strike as they have done at least 3-4 times previously with tear gas? Will the situation spiral out of control following its own internal logic?

At the same time certain PASOK MP's are alleging they won't vote for the 2nd round of IMF cuts and Standard and Poor has downgraded Greek govt bonds to below Ecuador and Jamaica.

Tue 14, June 2011 @ 11:17

Greek Parliamentary Blockade and 3rd General Strike in 2011 – 15th June 2011

Today was the day a general strike which was organised by the Greek GSEE-TUC, Adedy-Public Sector, and KKE-PAME (Communist Party). Alongside them were the alleged 'indignant' of Greece who had their usual drums and slogans 'Thieves, Thieves' 'Burn the Brothel (Parliament) Down'. These protests have been going on for 25 days today peacefully. Today they came under attack by a coordinated plan from black hooded provocateurs and the riot police which have used teargas extensively. Once again there were 3 different points of reference, one in Omonia by the KKE one in Pedion Arios by GSEE and one in Sindagma Sq.

Alongside the 'Indignant'
Many demonstrated gathered 7am in the morning trying to enforce the blockade round Parliament which is a very large area as on one side is the national park and on the other is the Presidential Palace. There were probably only around 5,000 at 7am and alongside a hundred or so we marched to block the entrance that would be the main focal point of the parliamentarians would use to get in. The actual entrance from the side of Sindagma Sq. was sealed off by police using a heavy metal barrier which had been placed on the road alongside two massive police buses. It was impossible to pass this route and as it was blocked by the police the parliamentarians couldn't get in. There were 32 police divisions in total 10,000. The largest for years and both Papandreou's car was attacked and the Presidents who are now meeting to decide whether he resigns and they go for new elections or a government of 'national unity'.
So a section of the demonstration agreed to march round the other

side of Parliament passing the national park and heading round the far end of roads which eventually will lead to Parliament. Despite there being only a couple of hundred the side roads were blocked but slowly more police started to arrive and a cat and mouse game occurred whereby the police created lines but they were outwitted by the demonstrators who went behind them at both points and continue to blockade the side roads. At some point riot police arrived with tear gas and they attacked the blockade picking on the vulnerable and those who tried to defend them arresting half a dozen. But in the meantime a couple of MP's cars were attacked and the police were criticised vehemently by what was said by protestors that they are defending 'traitors' and 'quislings' and that what happened in Keratea (where they were withdrawn after two months of struggle by the locals).

KKE Parliamentary Parade
On returning to Sindagma Square and going on to the KKE march one noticed that they were around 10,000 chanting the same old sterile slogans. This time they couldn't go round the front of Sindagma as it was occupied so they went down one side stayed outside the Ministry of Economics for a bit and the moment they started to leave the riot police at the other end of the square started to use tear gas. This type of gas is so powerful most people can't breathe but because many Greeks are well prepared people help each other with special sprays and lemons. One can't rub one's eyes with this type of tear gas even when one can't see.

Black hooded police provocateurs make their reappearance
For 25 days the demonstrators have been peaceful and now it appears the plan is to disperse the square violently as they have teargased everyone. Conflicts have now emerged amongst the indignant and the black hooded protestors thus giving an excuse that the demonstrators are all violent hoodlums to justify police attacks. So far there hasn't been one general strike which hasn't been dispersed by tear gas. Fires have started in the square where people are camped. But up till 4pm around 10,000 remain outside the main Sindagma Sq. and they haven't dispersed. What will happen over the next few hours and what the government will announce is still

fluid...

Evening
In total there must have been around 70-100,000 throughout the day on the streets in Athens. Three times attempts were made to disperse those on the main square and the battles raged from around 1.30pm till 5pm. Until 9pm one's eyes could still hurt from the teargas. After 7pm thousands started to arrive and by 9pm three quarters of Sindagma Sq. was full once more.

Throughout the day Papandreou met the leaders of all the main parties 5 in total (incl. the KKE) trying to unblock the political impasse of not being able to go forward to new elections (as the parties may get wiped out or end up 'governing' on such a small mandate to make it impossible) being unable to get agreement for a coalition government and Papandreou announcing that he would resign if some type of agreement could occur.

So he has now asked for a vote of confidence to form a 'new' government with him still as leader to gain some time to try and sell the 'new' appointments to pass the 2nd round of IMF measures on 28th June. His health minister Loverdos, who plans to cut the 140 hospitals for the IMF dictats stated that a bunch of hoodlums in the square can't dictate govt policy or the democratic nature of 'Parliament.

Having failed to throw out the protestors from the square with the use of known provocateurs many of which came directly out of government ministries and a couple were caught with their police ID on them by protestors and paraded on the internet, the govt has essentially fallen, the issue is what is to replace it and how can it sell IMF measures when everyone knows why it has fallen.

Some of the slogans heard tonight on the square:

-We aren't leaving the square the whole of Greece should become Keratea

-We will keep the ports and the Electricity company but sell the Parliamentary Brothel

-We will stay in the square take your provocateurs and Go Resign Resign Resign

-Bread Education Freedom the Junta didn't Die in 1973

-George (Papandreou) you are a Traitor and an American

-Resistance Resistance National Resistance

-Hellas Hellas Hellas

-Leonidas had 300 who had a soul we have 300 thieves, throw them in the sea so we have a Party

-Fxxx the IMF, where did the Money Go?

-Papulia Papulia (President) go tend to your vegetable garden

They chanted also against the Economics Minister Papakonstantinou to do one correct thing in his life and jump off a balcony, against Pangalos stating he should sell himself (as he is very fat) so we can pay off the debts

-We Owe No Money, We Aint Paying, We Have no Money

-The People United will Never be Defeated

On the Police:

-If you have Honour and you are Greek turn your police shields the other way to help us storm Parliament

-You get paid Peanuts to Beat People Up

-Police, Pigs, Murderers

The Deeper Meaning of the Victory in Sindagma Sq.

The events in Sindagma on 15th June constitute an undisputable fact. A fact that what has been born is a new subjective, which for the first time since November 1973 shows that with the aid of the proper moves and discussions, the time and experience to form a new deep and radical popular movement. For more than 5 hours, the broad popular masses of the 'indignant' of Sindagma Square, the new sans culottes of Athens, fought with persistence against all: the quisling government, its praetorian guards who didn't hesitate in throwing tonnes of teargas, even when they were just receiving sporadic plastic bottles and the black hooded goons who wanted to impose their own fetishism of violence against the broad masses of tens of thousands of people, trying to achieve what the govt wanted: For the squares to become empty, for people to go home and for the road to open towards the absolute sell out of the country. It didn't pass! For the first time since 1973, the people on their own, with the weapon being patience, with resolve and vigour, confronting the praetorians and armed black hooded dudes, imposed with its will and frightened all types of power. For a start they frightened the European partners, who saw in the militant Greek people the danger that it will provoke a broad pan-European domino of strong populist movements which will doubt the new Holy Alliance which they have set up. That is why they tried to transform – even after the events their stance -to stop even in the final moment this forceful revengeful mode with which they aimed to cripple our country irreversibly.

This shows that the popular movement with persistence and decisiveness can open the road to an essential and just negotiation for the future but not by these traitors and enemies of the people who represent us today. Secondly it frightened the occupying, quisling govt of Athens, That is why in a hurry and in a state of confusion which becomes ridiculous George Papandreou moved towards moves regarding 'compromise' in their ridiculous plans and did a rushed restructuring of the govt. A restructuring which brought out into the open the 'intensive care govt' to appear to be seats for right or left-wing seats to the alleged 'indignant' PASOK MP's, is aiming to silence their mouths and dampen down the rebellion inside PASOK to avoid the immediate dissolution of the party. From Wednesday onwards we have a PM whose back is up against the wall and we are the ones who have achieved this. As he knows that voting for the IMF Pt. 2 he will not have to do with the establishment and oppositionists inside Parliament but the solid wall of popular anger which does appear to be going calm. We have said it and we will say it again: the indignant, this broad popular mobilisation which one month now has convulsed the squares in Greece is a movement that comes from the future. It places a final gravestone to the misery of the establishment politics that have dominated since the end of junta. Either the establishment with ties which have sat on our necks and are openly selling our enslavement, or the 'establishment' doubters who for a long time had degenerated the last weapon of the people, a circus of pseudo-movements which were placed in the forefront due to their cosmopolitan world views and attacked the nation itself, its identity and its interests. The road to no return has started.

In Sindagma, in the White Castle (Thessaloniki) and in the other squares of Greece young old and all the INVISIBLE people of the Greek nation, we who for so many years had not voice and representatives anywhere to express our national and social issues for justice, our aims against this rotten world without morals and values are coming out of darkness and the remnants of the post-junta world. We are placing the Greek flag in the forefront and WE

WANT IT ALL: A new Greece and an independent society a proud people's national liberation social control ecology and direct democracy

ARDIN magazine-
RixisNewspaper
Ardin is one of the organisations that are involved in
Theodorakis movement Spitha....

One of the main banners in the square was **Vote for the IMF you win a Hanging** (Goudi-area where in history traitors of the Greek state were hanged!)

Continuous Eyewitness Account = 48Hour General Strike – Part One

When the Greeks demonstrate peacefully they dissolve him with teargas-State and Paramilitary state in alliance – Greek security services, Mossad, CIA- banner in the square ripped down...

Over the past week the situation has developed nightly with many people expressing their desperation at the situation and calling for more precise forms of direct action i.e. the storming of Parliament. From unemployed truckers to unemployed warehouse workers the desperation is seen on people's faces when they gather nightly to chant slogans and debate issues amongst speakers or themselves with other people in the square. Alongside this the govt via its Vice President declared a vote for the 2nd round of IMF measures has to occur or tanks will hit the streets' in the Spanish press El Mundo alongside a statement that all those who call for an exit from the Euro or a return to the Drachma are totally stupid.

The 4th General Strike this year has kicked off, with a shutdown in the ports, most of the public sector, timed electricity blackouts and the traditional two different demos starting from two different points. The KKE had left Sindagma Sq. by 11.30am this morning and they are supposed to come back this evening in order to repeat the same tomorrow when the vote goes through Parliament.

There is much confusion over the past week as to whether they will participate in the vote or if they withdraw they will hand the govt a victory as it will need less votes to pass through its IMF measures. The public sector unions around the Greek TUC and ADEDY have marched as well and many have stayed in Sindagma Sq. but so far it appears there are less people than last time as everyone has agreed to return in the evening. There have also appeared what appears to be black hooded characters who have massed at the bottom end of the square and last night an attempt was made by various parties to bring down the tents that have been there for one month now allegedly for health and safety reasons but most people have ignored them and aren't leaving.

. The peaceful nature of the protests reached their limit. More than 2 million Greeks gathered in squares and the end result was... worse IMF measures after the govt restructuring. The bankers and interest bearing bondholders need to paid. Soible stated that Greeks must give up even the sun. Everything else is to be sold off in a fire sale of immense proportions without an actual sale, but a giveaway. No wonder people chant Thieves to Prison for the Politicians in Parliament and a new banner has appeared stating the 'Biggest type of Violence is that of being Sacked and Unemployed'.

The circling of Parliament seems to have been a call made by a section of the demonstrators and a section of the media as well (with posters appearing with no organisational link to them) but done in such a manner whereby one would need around a million to cover all the entrances from the main roads instead of where the actual entrances are. In other words they are spreading people thin ensuring thus if the numbers don't show up, (how can they when there isn't a political organisation that can control this) their actions won't have the actual desired effect. Coupled with the role of the KKE which marches separately and leaves the scene just as teargas is fired, the new 48hour general strike (which hasn't occurred ever since the fall of the Junta) we have had a new situation developing.

Alongside that has been the massive media attention now to default and what has occurred in other countries from Russia to Argentina to Iceland. The worlds press has been present in Greece since the 15th June and the issue is why? Since 1985 Greece has paid back

E865billion and its economy doesn't add up to more than 2% of EU GDP. All the new measures don't reduce the actual size of the foreign debt but magnify it by attacking working class living standards directly and indirectly.

Coaches are coming from many parts of Greece and many of the demonstrators this morning seem to be well prepared with gas masks and sea goggles for the eventual tear gas attacks. The mood appears to be that something will kick off, but we don't know exactly when.

2pm

Afternoon and Evening Events

Between 2-6pm the known black hooded police provocateurs started to attack police lines not anywhere near Parliament but at either end of the square giving the riot police the excuse to tear gas everyone away from the main squares as all that remained apart from the 'indigenous' were the leftist groups. Most people left in order to come back in the evening during the Parliamentary debates. At some point the riot police teargased both entrances of the Sindagma metro so people who were inside could choke and many did as women with young children ended up needing to be hospitalised.

KKE – PAME arrives in order to depart from jeering crowds

At around 7pm the KKE via its union leadership PAME arrived at the top end of the square right in front of Parliament and most people greeted them that finally they had come to join the common struggle against the IMF. They have a very large truck with many loudhailers and this was parked right in the middle in the square and it is usual for the KKE never to be a minority and when it holds its own meetings in squares talks only to itself so to be in an area as just another organisation was too much for its organisers. So when they started to depart people started jeering them and a few scuffles broke out. Many shouted shame or clapped ironically saying also well done, the parade is over. During arguments with the KKE stewards their complaint was that if they arrive on the square (one month after this movement started) people don't want them and if they leave people jeer at them. This is obviously quite logical as the KKE criticised those who were on the squares when they said the struggle is only in the factories when ironically they had always stated people should hit the streets against the economic measures and when they did they told them to go back to the factories (as if everyone is working!!) What was clearly discernible was that the volume of people on the streets has affected the KKE and it can no longer pretend its policies are actually serving any other purpose than a left cover for IMF-PASOK

Tear gas for 5 hours straight-but people don't go away

After the KKE left the motorbike contingent against the IMF arrived in the square to the crowds who clapped in support and soon thereafter the riot police started a 5 hour barrage of tear gas and little rocket bombs that make a massive amount of noise to shake you and a little explosion. People started to defend themselves and throw water bottles at police lines and anything they could find, but the volume of teargas was so intense that even if you had gasmasks and sea goggles the smoke alone meant it was difficult to see, but at least you could breathe. During lulls in the conflict two individuals climbed over the police barriers and confronted the riot police on their own. The shouting and screaming at the police was constantly interspersed with slogans of Police, Pigs, and Murderers which thronged the whole square and Hellas Hellas. Despite the volume of tear gas the people never dispersed just retreated as the police fired tear gas straight at you and you could be seriously injured by the teargas canister. Fires were lit in the square below and aids were handing out Maalox (chemical compound for bad stomach diluted) spray for the burning eyes.
28/06/11
At the same time this morning a minister stated Greece will not be Argentina when by all accounts this is the beginning as the old order is disintegrating and by teargas alone one cannot keep such a large mass of people in check. To what extent people today will accept to be attacked by the police indefinitely without counterattacking in the known ways (Molotov cocktails etc.) may be the marvels or our 'modern era'. At the same time the 'Special Olympics' are occurring which have cost around 100million. There are more than 15,000 police who have been on duty now for around 2 days straight and thousands of protestors are arriving from many parts of Greece. The battle begins anew.
29/06/11
 VN Gelis

Athens Burns in IMF Induced Teargas Hell

Continuous Eyewitness Account: Part 2-48 Hour General Strike

Whilst the govt's IMF package Mk2 passed with 155 votes and just as the KKE's parade ended the police using its riot police launched a brutal teargas war with the hundred odd thousand in the main square. Tear gas was thrown right in the middle of crowds right above the heads of protestors, Chinese made bomb sounding pellets were also thrown to create maximum confusion and panic. But the protestors didn't panic. They stood firm, as most were prepared with gas masks and sea goggles to avoid the effects of the tear gas which is stinging eyes and burning sensation in all skin surfaces left uncovered. Alongside the tear gas they threw gas which meant you couldn't also breathe. Brute force without the use of police provocateurs was the order of the day after they had a trial run the night before.

More than 500 people were injured, the police wanting to disperse the top end of Sindagma Sq. also in order to ensure the bottom end of the square sections of which are funded directly by the Ford Foundation and Soros in the USA weren't to be left out. By dispersing the bottom end of the square they revealed that their aim was to show that a banana republic has to crush all resistance to the IMF in order to prove to the banksters that have them on the payroll as to what a good protectorate they are. What they achieved on the ground, they lost in the spirit of the people, who faced the riot police unarmed, with plastic water bottles and their arms.

Whilst the battles lasted for up to 8 hours yesterday and the riot police must have thrown the equivalent of 6 months use of tear gas, they created another set of problems. By dispersing the crowds they set them further afield at least half a mile from the centre and created at least five zones of conflict. Pavements were ripped up and the marble was broken to be used as rocks against the riot police. Fires were set at the central Post Office, the Economics Ministry at a certain 4x hotel, phone booths and bus stations. For hours the youth fought and the riot police returned the rocks throwing them back. At various times they brought the mobile police units on motorbike that drove past the crowds on the side streets and they threw tear gas at them. They even attacked people eating in restaurants and in cafes who didn't necessarily have anything to do with the demo. They threw tear gas into the main metro station right where there was a standby area for injured people creating a gas storm ensuring the injured became even more injured and hoping that someone may die.

During the day two members of Parliament were attacked (one a member of the KKE and another member of PASOK). The political situation has now changed irrevocably beyond the pale. The peaceful nature of the protests so far reached their limit. One cannot confront the praetorian guards of the IMF with plastic water bottles or with bare hands. The IMF hasn't usually departed peacefully anywhere on earth. It arrives sucks the blood out of the people leaves behind chaos disaster and despair and provokes rebellion. It appears what happened in Athens yesterday was the last chance for the IMF to leave peacefully. It didn't happen. Next time the parliamentary junta will be overthrown and the 300 Quisling MP's will be thrown out. People learn quickly in Greece. In the first six months of the IMF 80's abstained from local elections, and in another six months 2 million took to the squares. In the next six months they will chase and hound every politician wherever they are, their local offices, their electoral offices, they will refuse to pay for all the new tax rises and they will confront the IMF banksters head on.

As they say on the square with the large banner and the slogans they chanted against the riot police

Bread Peace Freedom, the Junta Didn't Die in 1973
In this square we will Bury the IMF

From words to deeds will be the next phase. Just as in the Russian
Revolution the masses unorganised demonstrated in their thousands
with peaceful intentions against the Tsar and were met brutally head
on by the praetorian guards of the era, so in our times, the IMF will
be buried in Greece. We witnessed the future in the events of
yesterday and it is clear the people can no longer be ruled and those
who rule can no longer rule in the old way. Greece will be reborn on
the ashes of the IMF, the EU and the Euro.

Greece belongs to the Greeks and will remain so despite the
giveaway nature of the new measures. For that no one who
demonstrated had a different opinion and the mood of the masses
wasn't one of defeatism, but resistance till victory.

June 2011
VN Gelis

Taxi Drivers on Indefinite Strike Against IMF Liberalisation Measures

For three weeks now Greek taxi drivers have been on strike against the neo-liberal measures of the IMF and the quisling PASOK government. They have had marches, blockades of ports and airports and have essentially bypassed their elected representatives. In Crete, at Iraklion airport the taxi drivers blockaded the airport for 5 hours, teargas was fired and conflict ensued. North and South Greece was cut off due to the blockade at Rio-Antirio. PASOK offices have been attacked in Northern Greece and have been destroyed.

Many taxi drivers at least 25% have paid around E200k for their licences. The govt announced overnight that their licences are to be worth zero and they would issue new licences for a small sum. There are already 14,000 licences many of which are also fake and don't actually have a licence to operate and due to the economic crisis takings have been reduced significantly. The destruction of their licences without the state undertaking to buy them out has pushed taxi drivers to the edge. They have adopted the tactics and strategy of a generalised guerrilla war with the govt in the middle of summer right bang in the middle of the tourist season. When large cruise ships with 5-10k passengers are unable to dock in Piraeus, or no taxis can be found from one end of Greece to the other, this shows a level of commitment which hasn't been seen so far by any other section. The taxi drivers meet daily and decide on the spot what type of action to take thus bypassing the leadership. Indeed today Limberopoulos the leader of the taxi drivers stated we cannot control their reactions essentially stating that he condemns their form of resistance as after all the leaders of all the traditional leaderships are allied with existing political parties of formations and were brought into those positions in the pre-IMF era. With the governmentt reshuffle during the events in June (protests by Indignant and 3 general strikes culminating in the battle of Athens) which convulsed Greece a new minister of Transport took over called Rangousis and he sought fit to crush the taxi-drivers in the middle of the summer season gambling on the fact that if they are defeated that will open the way for the liberalisation of all the closed professions as dictated by the IMF-EU.

The bankruptcy of the Left is highlighted once more as they are spectators of an unfolding drama in the struggle of the Greek taxi drivers. If they are defeated, companies will take over many of the taxis and the drivers will become salaried employees many of whom in order to keep the wages to a bare minimum will end up being recently arrived immigrants and the taxi drivers will suffer the same fate as suffered by farmers, truckers before them. Apart from verbal messages of support the KKE abstains. The Euros on the other hand openly condemned the forms of struggle of the taxi drivers in Parliament saying it doesn't do justice to their struggle. One of the taxi drivers slogans has been 'with blood we gained our licences, with blood we will give them away' 'taxi drivers are here united and strong' (paraphrasing an old PASOK slogan)

Postscript
The taxi drivers like the truckers before them were eventually sold out by their leaders. Union leaders who belong to the previous generation of sellouts committed either to the ruling PASOK gov't or the KKE. 13 regionally leaders without a vote from the base decided to end the strike whilst 6 voted for a continuation with Thessaloniki voting for as well.
July 2011VN Gelis

Drachma or Euro? Default on Way

For the corrupt mass media a return to the Drachma equals destruction! For what reason they don't say. It is served as an honour and explanations don't exist. It is destruction, because it is ...destruction, pure and simple!

"Catastrophic for Greece was how it was characterised by a journalist Ev Mitilinaios the scenario of returning to the drachma" we read in the VIMA newspaper, without anywhere the argument being justified.

The same goes for Papariga (leader of the KKE) who actually doesn't tire in warning us: "A return to the drachma under the current conditions would be catastrophic"!
The why and how must be held only for themselves.

Also the European specialists speak about destruction but we understand them e.g. The president of the European central bank, Z. C. Trichet who supports that it will be: destructive for the Eurozone the return to the drachma. He doesn't say this for Greece. We would agree with him, with the meaning that a departure of Greece from the Eurozone would mean the end of an opportunist, stupid and criminal attempt to impose a united currency without a united economy and state. The responsibility belongs to the architects of the EU and the Eurozone, with the victim being Greece and the other countries of the European South.

There are others who state that due to the lack of a similar experience, the honest reply to the question as to 'what will happen if we return to the drachma' is simply, 'I don't know'!

We Have Experience

In reality there is experience not from one but many countries. Typically they aren't the same, but essentially they don't differ. Before we analyse things more, let us give a hypothetical preliminary example so one can be better understood:
Let us assume we had held onto the drachma but had latched it onto a hard currency, something which isn't at all rare in international practice, e.g. the Euro. Whoever gave us one drachma we would give them back one euro. That is what happened in the beginning of the 1990's with the Argentinian peso. So as to be confronted, they said, inflation would be added to the dollar. One peso=one dollar and the opposite. This occurred with the bright sparks down at the IMF!

The Results are Well Known.

The problem of the Argentinian economy was found in its currency? A big deceit. A case of fetishism, which we come across only in the field of religion. Where the painter of holy images paints Mary and falls down on his feet in front of his piece of art and asks for himself to be saved! Thus man in society and commercial production has lot from his eyes his true relationships with his co-citizens and the division of labour among them, due to common survival and fantasizes that his life is determined not by the relationship with his co-workers but by other creations e.g. from a printed piece of paper, like the peso, which in and of itself has minimal value.

The diagnosis is wrong and the medicine chosen also. The patient wasn't the typed piece of paper as is always to be believed by monetarist bourgeois economics but in the given situation the low level of competition of the Argentinian economy in the international arena. The medicine chosen for the peso to become as hard as the dollar, without having in the background the dynamism of the US economy, the only thing it could achieve was to destroy totally the competitiveness of the Argentinian economy. As exactly happened.

Argentina had to travel backwards; its peoples had to suffer for a decade, to go bankrupt essentially for 75% of the debt to be written off, to disconnect the peso from the dollar and for it to be devalued, for the economy to start to develop once more. Naturally the problem wasn't solved permanently as the Argentinian economy is part of the world economy and in conditions of world crisis they cannot but influence all the national economies. The abandonment of the policy of the hard currency in Argentina ended up being the correct and imposed choice.

With Greece before WW2 the same had occurred. Venizelos as well in the name of anti-inflationary targets latched the drachma onto the British pound and later onto the dollar. As a result imports made money instead of exports; the deficits grew alongside the debts. Venizelos (no relation to current Economics Minister!) responded with an intensification of direct taxation, with sackings, cuts, autarchy and violence. In 1932 the country was forced to declare bankruptcy, taking the drachma off the link with the dollar and devaluation. Due to the policy that he followed the Liberal party imploded and Venizelos was forced to junk in his political career. From his ridiculous insistence on the hard drachma the political duet of Glyxbourg (ex-King) – Metaxas whilst the dictatorship that followed led the borrowers that Greece would continue to pay its debts.

Like Argentina in our days, Greece not only did not destroy itself, as the pre-war Cassandra's predicted but with a weapon the national monetary policy and its refusal to continue to pay this odious debt, it added phenomenal rhythms of development taking on the third highest on the planet after Japan and the Soviet Union!

What is the difference of coming out of a link with whatever hard currency (or from the hard Euro – if that was the relationship) from the forced or chosen exit from the Eurozone? None whatsoever. Let them not say that there isn't a historical parallel that we don't have experience and we don't know what the consequences are going to be for a return to our national currency.

I have referred to two examples but there are tens of others. Let those who sell catastrophism sell it to those who have no clue. We will not allow Greece and the Greek nation to disappear so some can sell slavery to the Euro-Atlantic bosses defending either which way the condemned Eurozone.

Unfounded Catastrophist Syllogisms

In the press and the internet one finds syllogisms against the return of the drachma, but one doesn't find many arguments. That isn't a coincidence. I haven't searched extensively but to the extent that I did, I found four paragraphs by Petros Dukas with which he tries to convince us that a return to the Drachma will be catastrophic. For all those that don't realise relatively that he was Deputy Minister in two New Democracy govts, he studied economics and international relations in George Washington University, company management and finance economics at Columbia University and economics in New York University, to which he became a doctor of Economics. He also worked for Citibank in New York and became the general manager for the same bank in Greece.

P. Dukas supports that:
"The discussion and the threatening dilemma for a return to the drachma are unintelligible and self-destructive for our country. Further down he posts the first attack we will be forced to accept as Greeks!
The points numbered are Dukas the answers are mine.

1) We will constitute acceptance that us Greeks have totally failed, that we are unable to compete and we are in the 3rd Division of Europe

As Greeks were never asked or questioned if they wanted Greece to become a member of the EEC. Any who had a basic understanding knew that Greece was being thrown into a wolves den, as without trade protectionism it was impossible to compete with the west-European mega giants, when essentially, without the nations being asked, the rule of common market preference on the basis which the Union occurred, never functioned as this is how the uncontrolled centres of power in Brussels decided. Even worse there never were any European trade boundaries. With the GATT agreements and later the WTO ones the European market was transformed officially into a united world market, without the nations being asked. The entrance of Greece in 2001 into the Eurozone was the last nail in the coffin of the Greek economy. The fate of the Greek economy had been judged and that was known by all our politicians (amongst which is Dukas) unless of course we are to accept they are chosen simply by the level of dumbness.

2) The 'New Drachma' would unavoidably become immensely devalued in order to be able to aid the competitiveness of our exports. But never before has devaluation had anything more than medium term successes. It led to a cycle of inflation, a fear of a new devaluation, exit of capital and finally new devaluations.

Above the doctor of economics and deputy minister of economics (let us not forget that one) tells us that "we failed totally, that we are unable to become competitive and we are falling into the 3rd Division" But in paragraph 2 we accepted that the devalued drachma will "aid the competitiveness of exports" and consequently accepts that the overvalued for Greek measures euros will undermine our competitiveness. This doesn't stop him arguing (totally illogically) that the return of the drachma is destruction! He must assume that he is talking to idiots…

Fear Mongering Nonsense

Where does it come from that the devalued drachma equal's inflation? Or that more inflation brings about more inflation and that is why we will have capital flight abroad? All of this isn't but nonsense with which our esteemed Dr. is trying to frighten the people.

Inflation develops when we have few goods in the market in relation with demand hence we have an increase in prices. Or when the country is forced to print money from air as it has created obligations where its actual government coffers aren't able to service.

The new drachma will be devalued in relation not to itself but from its original price 1Euro=340.75Drachma s which it was on 1st January 2001. Not because it is written in its DNA but because it is to the interest of the country. It must because Greece became an open border paradise and lost all its rights handed over to foreign centres of power with the Euro hanging on its neck and lost as a result 50% of its competitiveness.

There will be repercussion which will occur on life, but they will only be positive. If the German Euro can't be devalued for the Greek terrain, the quislings that rule us found the answer in devaluing our lives. How else are we going to feed the usurers and we save the Eurozone which is one step away from death! They are taking the last cent which is circulating in the country having provoked a depression, mass unemployment, they cut and cut again salaries, pensions, they have unleashed a fierce tax chasing mechanism, the make incessant and constant increases in fuel, the prices of all utilities, the prices of all the basic basket of goods, they destroy the welfare state, all the services linked to people, health, education, everything.

The "New Drachma" which will replace the Euro will have the same form one euro = one new drachma which should become a paper note, with the same subdivisions and paper multipliers so as to avoid whatever speculation against the consumers. Whatever could be bought with one euro should be bought with one drachma. A wage of 800 Euros will become a wage of 800drachmas. The necessary devaluation is related to the relationship of the drachma with the euro and foreign currencies. In 2001 it was 1E=340drachma. Due to the economic meltdown which the country has suffered whose fault is due to the corrupt political personnel this relationship will change in defence of the drachma if we want to promote our exports and tourism. 1 Euro can become = 440.75drachmas. This devaluation in relation to foreign currencies is obviously going to influence to an extent the internal prices of the market, but not in a country where the govt will utilise all the possibilities internally and our relationships with abroad. We must add that a return to a drachma on its own does not satisfy for the country to stand on its feet. It must constitute the beginning of a new course, the independent and national domination of Greece, ready for new openings and open to fruitful co-operations with new peoples all over the planet, on the basis of mutual gain alone.

To proceed further: which exit of capital and fear of inflation is Dukas talking about? There are around $350 billion euros and dollars in the bank of Greece. There are the trading reserves of the country and not one has the right to touch them. If the state has the will it is in the position of defending them. Let us forget about capital flight. Neither Argentina in our days nor Greece in 1932 confronted such issues with bankruptcy and will not confront them now. The planet as a whole is facing the most complicated the most explosive crisis in its history and there are no areas which are now secure for any currency in any country. If capital flight occurs in Turkey which has its own currency the same will occur in Greece...

3) The massive debt in Euros should be paid in devalued drachmas. As a result our debt will increase to around 250% of GDP! Will the doctor of economics drive us mad: Given the fact that the 'massive debt' won't anyway be paid back (everyone understands that) not only is the debt transformed into drachmas but so does the GDP. Therefore the relationship of debt to GDP, remains constant, it doesn't change because we change currency.

4) All the citizens with investments and deposits in our country would aim to avoid the losses incurred from a return to a Drachma and would take out quickly all the capital abroad with the result being the immediate collapse of the banking system and economic activity!

The respect and worth of a currency of a country is determined by the productivity of work but also by the quality of the productive goods. It improves or deteriorates from the development of these two factors. If they impose a currency on you like the Euro whose respectability and its price in the markets is very high as it is based on German competitiveness and quality, then it is truly illogical and an unnatural situation as it weakens severely exports, as he accepts in the 2nd paragraph and supports imports. With the Euro Greece has a permanent date with bankruptcy. We need a 180degree turn and one of the first measures for the country on the road to development is a return to a cheap drachma. When that occurs we won't have capital flight or investments from the country. The New Democracy 'doctor of economics' deceives aims to influence the Greek people. With the cheap drachma capital will flood into the country. If the opposite occurred as is being alleged we wouldn't see American and European capital emigrating to China with the cheap Renminbi but Chinese, Korean and Taiwanese to be emigrating to Western Europe and the USA!

As for the banks we say going bankrupt one after the other from the epidemic in the USA and Un Kingdom that occurred not because of capital flight abroad (so as to find safe ports, where truly?) but because we have a lack of liquidity, as their reserves are 'toxic' they are obligations by debtors who cannot pay. That is why every now and again states are making injections of liquidity in the banks so as to keep alive the money of its citizens. That occurs because it is in the nature of the market (which has been deliberately deified) cutting things down to size or increasing as it sees fit. The market is a creation of man and his creation; it cannot regulate the life of its creator. The creator man will tomorrow regulate the market and thus his life.

www.patari.org
August 2011

Appendix: Historical Background

Editor's Note: Two historical articles which encapsulate both the history of the region, in particular the last great occupation of Greece and the recent machinations of the New World Order in the Balkans with Yugoslavia once at the epicentre

The Last Great Speech of Aris Velouhiotis
Leader of EAM-Greek National Liberation Movement against the German Occupation of WW2

WHY I FOUGHT

On 19th October Lamia is liberated. The forces of ELAS, representatives of PEEA and EAM arrive in the city. On 29th October after the celebration of the NO (Greek repulsion of Italian invasion of 1940 into Albania) a meeting is held in the main square, Freedom for EAM to celebrate the victory in WW2 with a presence of the whole district of Pamfthiotida.

Aris gives his most famous speech ever from the balcony of a hotel. Brothers — Greek men and women of Lamia and the region — I bring warmest greetings from the General Headquarters of ELAS. As you will have observed, I am about to make a speech. But this speech will not be like the speeches you have heard before from the old party chiefs; I will not promise, as they promised, to build bridges or make rivers flow. I cannot promise you the world, and I do not wish to ply you with rhetoric; I wish only that you hear what I have to say. I will begin with a fairytale. The immortal Greek race.

Once the part of this land called Greece in which we stand was glorious and happy. It produced a culture which for two-and-a-half-thousand years has been admired all over the world. Never has a word been written by the wise or the unwise that is not first attested in the works left by the creators of this ancient Greek civilization. Once, therefore, our country was glorious; but it was later enslaved and its former glory lost. After many years, our country found its feet again. After a hard struggle against slavery, it was liberated once more. With the era of slavery came hardness and darkness. For many years 'intellectuals', among them a certain, Fallmeyer claimed that the Greek race had been extinguished and that its place had been usurped by other peoples who held nothing in common with the ancient Greek race. But this claim was proved false. The proof was Hellenism, and with this proof our country rose again victorious and free. Neither foreign kings nor local landowners wanted a free and victorious Greece . Afraid of the French Revolution and its consequences, foreign kings created among themselves the Holy Alliance to suppress insurrection. The local landowners were in alliance with the Turks, and together they robbed the Greek people. Reaction screeches The Greek people would not be Greeks — the people of these lands of freedom and civilization — but a people of the jungle if they failed to produce leaders who would lead them to freedom. Knowing this, oppressors foreign and local fought against the Greeks to prevent them from rebelling and so gaining their freedom. During the years of slavery the struggle — on a scale great or small, under arms or without — was waged unceasingly.

From the Greek people emerged a sweeping revolutionary movement lent impetus by its songs, by the idea of the insurrection of the nation and by Rigas Feraios, precursor of the Friendly Society. Slain by the forces of reaction before he could bring his principles into action, the seed Rigas Feraios sowed grew rapidly; before long the Friendly Society became a fact. It had thousands of Greek followers.

And the forces of reaction screeched! They signed deceitful treaties such as that which emerged from the Congress of Vienna in 1815; Ioannis Kapodistrias was one of these signatories. Under this treaty, the forces of reaction would first support the national liberation struggle if it broke out in Greece , only to strangle it later.

Kapodistrias, who is presented in schools as a great and important man through the display of his portraits and speeches, was the first destroyer of Greece. However, he did what he did not as Kapodistrias but as a representative of Greek reaction. It was in this role that he screeched alongside international and local reaction; it was in this role that he signed deceitful treaties.

The people advance Nothing was able to contain the fire of freedom that burned in the hearts of our people. In 1821, after many trials and tribulations, they followed the flame of Papaflessas — who used all means, even lies in declaring an insurrection. So it was that the revolution began in the area of Morea in 1821. At the declaration of this insurrection the powerful of the earth, foreign and local alike, became frightened. The local traitors, seeing the impossibility of containing the people and frightened by their rage, were forced to end their collaboration with the occupiers and to take part in the popular national liberation movement with the aim of corrupting it. The movement against the revolution took on an international character. The powerful of the earth were frightened. They used all their trickery to try to crush the revolution. But they failed. For seven whole years our forebears fought, despite the fact that twice — in 1823 and 1825 — the forces of reaction in Greece organised a civil war in an attempt to break the struggle. Thus it was that our forebears forced all our enemies to suck where once they had spat; to recognise our struggle and our independence. Previously no one had believed that this miracle could be achieved by our own forces and our own people. Some waited for freedom to come from Russia ; others put their hope in the benevolence of the kings of Europe . But the revolution proved that it and it alone was capable of providing freedom for our country. The myth of Philhellenism, through which we are alleged to have achieved our freedom, was invented so it would appear that our country was freed not by dint of its own native strength but by that of foreigners. There were, of course, those friendly to the Greeks —Philhellenes — who fought and spilt blood for the freedom of our country. Honour and glory are due them for their aid to our nation. But they were isolated individuals acting on their own; the theory of organised Philhellenism is a myth.

THE POPULAR CHARACTER

In the midst of the victory of the revolution, traitors still dominated our country. The forces of reaction, domestic and foreign, used all available means in their attempts to corrupt the popular character of the revolutionary movement and impose a new regime of slavery. In the end they achieved this. The initiator was Ioannis Kapodistrias, the man I spoke of earlier; but later, another Ioannis — Ioannis Metaxas — would attempt to finish the work that Kapodistrias had begun.

The people believed that once they had achieved the revolution years of brilliance would follow; the whole of humanity would be on their side and our country would again guide humanity down new paths of civilisation and progress. Instead, local and foreign forces of reaction imposed themselves, bringing with them Kapodistrias and the Bavarian Dynasty in place of the Ottomans

Many years of deceit and corruption held us back from progress and civilisation and threw us instead into desperation, hunger, immiseration and distihia. Thus Greece, which was once the source of light and civilisation, sunk to the lowest level of economic and social and cultural development not merely in the Balkans but in the whole of Europe .

THE BETRAYAL OF THE ALBANIAN EPIC

The essence of this backwardness is to be found in the fact that the forces of reaction directed their energies towards the torture and exploitation of those who organised popular movements, the cultivation of conflict within those movements and the propagation among the people of the idea that it was their lot to live in poverty. Taking their cue from Kolokotronis, who said that that our country is an 'impoverished beggar', the reactionaries managed to convince the Greek people that they could not stand on their own two feet; that they must be governed by foreigners. So the reactionaries called upon the Powers — the Russians, the English and the French. It was to this that our rulers had brought us. Later, we were to achieve democracy, but only because of the struggles of the people. The snake may shed its skin, but it remains a snake. The forces of reaction found democracy at fault for the misery of the people and turned once again to the monarchy. They brought back the king and commenced more brazenly to exploit the people. To silence the people's screams they imposed upon us Metaxas, who had been an agent of the German High Command ever since he studied at the German military academy. Thus it was that after 120 years we fell into slavery again, so badly had we been governed during those years. It was in this situation that we found ourselves when a war against the two colossi began to threaten.

But no one thought about how our country could escape the destruction that war would bring; instead, knowing that this country was headed for destruction, we entered the war.

We have documents proving that our rulers intended to make merely a token effort in the Albanian epic and then hand Greece over to the fascists. We have documents which prove that during November and December 1940 we Greeks could have driven the Italians into the sea; but our rulers instead kept the army restrained until they could use Germany's victories in Europe to justify the argument that Greece was unable to fight both the colossi. They didn't trust in the magnificence of our army; neither in its courage, its fearlessness, its self-denial nor its heroism, even though, hungry and shoeless in the mountains of Albania, it had fought against fascism with great ferocity and the aid of the Greek people.

That is how they bound us once more to slavery.

Our people were no longer in a position to continue their resistance, however fervent their feelings. Even with their ardour, our people were unable to hold back the assault by the metallic giant of fascism after they had been sold out and betrayed by their leaders. Although the people were obliged to submit, they were not defeated, since the capitulation was signed before the army had even fought. Thus the defeat was suffered not by our people but by the regimes which had ruled them between 1821 and 1941. Our people are today are in the process of turning this defeat into victory — a victory that becomes ever more complete with the progress of time.

In such a way did the Germans arrive in our land and turn us into slaves. But our people would not abandon their country, and the blemish of defeat disappeared when we rebelled. And what did we get from those who wore the "clak and bakaliarika?" The only thing they could find to tell us was:

"Keep calm and silent. Maintain order. We have established a government; calm down."

In this, they reflected the will of the Germans. Such words were spoken by those who have no right to be called Greek; but they could not compromise the honour of our nation, of which our people are the guardians.

And yet two and a half months later the noise of the guns began. What words were spoken then? As in 1821 the forces of reaction conspired against us. In the beginning, they said nothing about the guerrilla war; they ignored it. They did as the ostrich does when it buries its head in the sand while the rest of its body remains visible. They thought that if they said nothing about the guerrilla war and ignored it the commotion of war would cease. But it did not cease, and every day the mountains were stained red with blood.

As the guerrilla war escalated and their silence proved incapable of stopping it, the reactionaries changed tack; they set themselves to fight us. They labelled us crooks, animal thieves, gangsters and so on. They even found people to condemn us because we killed the traitor and blackmailer Marathea. These people were totally stupid; they couldn't even recognise that which was in their own interests. They assumed that, if they attacked and disassociated themselves from us, our struggle would cease and we would never be capable of tightening the noose round their necks.

So be it; they were stupid then and they spoke their stupidities aloud. Let them now eat their words.

THE COUNTRYSIDE IS BREATHING.

How did this happen? The villagers saw for the first time that they could safely leave their possessions outside in the open without their being tampered with. Animal thieving had been eradicated in the countryside and security of life and property was as it had never been before. Was this a miracle? No. But for the first time the people of the villages were in a position of power from which they could fight back against betrayal, animal theft and other crimes and replace them with security.

When we mounted our assault on these crimes and on betrayal, the reactionaries, like women of the aristocracy who refuse to see the human misery and impoverishment around them and instead concern themselves with the illness of a stray cat, raised their voices and condemned us on the grounds that we kill. Under Metaxas, women were raped; thousands of people were martyred; many were killed and thrown from balconies by the security services. So many crimes were committed, even against the old. Yet none among the reactionaries spoke up. And now they screech, 'Aris kills!'

Yes, we have killed before and are ready to kill again if need be. Who did we kill? We have bigger hearts than they. The proof of this is that we were the ones who were beaten up and hunted down over the years. We slaughtered those who betrayed the Greeks to the occupiers —those who stole from the people and committed crimes.

Those who believe that they suffered pain when we justifiably attacked them are ridiculously stupid, so as to side with them or they are wholeheartedly partners in crime. Neither did this trick work either .

THE GUERRILLA WAR SAVES THE PEOPLE

And then the forces of reaction developed a perfect formulation: 'We have no objection to the guerrillas' carrying out a national struggle, but the question is to be resolved by the big powers. What, then, is the purpose of struggling and dying? The matter will be resolved by outsiders!

The reactionaries found success with this formulation. Was it correct? Of course not! And this is why:

In 1941-42 EAM was not yet very strong. That is why the struggle had not yet taken on a mass character; neither was EAM conducting guerrilla activity. In 1941-42 approximately 300,000 people died from hunger and disease in Athens , Piraeus and the surrounding villages alone, and even more would have died had EAM not mobilized the people through demonstrations, meetings and strikes. Through these, the people were given the courage to stop the looting of our production by a section of the occupiers, to leave the feeding of the people to the International Red Cross and to observe the situation of Greece internationally.

If the guerrilla war had not prevented the Germans from stealing our production by ending the concentration on production of goods that the occupiers favoured the number of victims of hunger and disease would have been much higher.

When have we ever heard in the history of humanity that liberation can be achieved using backhanded methods? Never. Freedom isn't achieved with prayers but with struggle and suffering!

But even had we wanted, we didn't have the right to blacken the history of our country. That would be disrespect to the memory of our heroic ancestors.

Neither did we have the right to implant the stamp on the forehead of the forthcoming generations, our children and our grandchildren, that they originate from a land of eunuchs who agreed to die on the streets from the most vile of deaths — from hunger — instead of dying with gun in hand fighting for freedom.

What should we prefer? The first or the second? We answer a thousand times with no shadow of doubt: TO FIGHT!

Better for everything to burn down instead of us capitulating to the occupiers.

This our people realised, turning their backs on the quislings and thus gave the heroes of ELAS their victories.

REACTION CONSPIRES

This forced EKKA to change tune and take their own guerrilla forces into the mountains.

But why did they do this?

EAM had declared that it doesn't have a monopoly on guerrilla struggle. That's why it called on EKKA to create common guerrilla groups. If they had the desire to fight against the occupiers they would have done it spontaneously. But then they used to argue that the geography of Greece and the lack of space due to the occupation did not allow the existence of guerrilla groups.

But when they saw us liberate the country they then decided to create a guerrilla army.

What would anyone accept from them as being the guiding principle? What slogan would come out of their mouths? Naturally 'Down with the Occupiers'. But they clarified their position from the beginning.

Their first scream was: "Down with EAM"!

But we still called on them to unite. They refused, as they didn't want to get their hands dirty and to struggle to fight the occupier. They weren't implementing the will of the Greek people, but of reaction frightened by peoples' democracy and they set out to fight it.

In the end they declared war on us, with arms, collaborating with the occupiers.

We would not be consistent in our struggle and betrayers of the people if we hated blood. That is why, as followers of the will of the people, we crushed these collaborators of the occupiers, those who fought against our national struggle.

ELAS ON THE SIDE OF THE ALLIES

Then they used another trick: they condemned us as not supporting the Allied struggle and that we were the tools of the Russians. They threatened us that when the Allies came here they would sort us out: they who collaborated with the Germans had the gall to threaten us that the Allies would attack us!

They who in 1941 betrayed the Allied struggle! They who allowed the Three Hundred to be left alone in Thermopylae by leaving the Allied English to fight alone whilst they had surrendered the country with the quisling role of Tsolagoglou condemned for not aiding the allied struggle and they placed in the minds of the Allies that they would attack us on coming here.

GORGOPOTAMOS

But very soon the first slap arrived for them! The first group of English parachutists came not to them but to Aris in the Giona area. Alongside them we blew up the Gorgopotamos bridge. The leader of the Allied armies in the Middle East, General Wilson declared that 80% of the success of the Allies in Africa was due to the blowing up of the Gorgopotamos bridge as this stopped the sending of German war supplies and support. And one more thing: in the Peloponnese we proposed to the tsoliades (rightists) that they lay down their arms and we would let them go free. But the English refused this and arrested all the tsoliades, locked them up in concentration camps and advised they should be tried in military courts (as quislings — translators note). In the end we have the English with us. They are going down the streets of Lamia and they are going to attack the Germans with us. We will fight alongside them and not against them until the total defeat of fascism.

But we are being attacked now by a new argument. We are being condemned as being all communists and they are stating that EAM and ELAS are Communist Front organisations. But can this category constitute shame or glory?

WE ARE FIGHTING FOR DEMOCRACY

The Communist Party isn't now fighting for communism. In its programme the KKE has Communism as its final aim. But not for now. Communism will be imposed by the people, not the KKE. I am sure that many of those educated fellows who don't want it today, will in future vote so as to ensure that communism dominates.

But today the KKE does not aim at that but at a democratic solution to the Greek problem.

But let us say that the KKE were to implement Communism. They say that Communism destroys the churches and skins alive the priests. Are Communists so stupid that they will destroy the churches, which do not disturb us in any way.

WHO ATTACKS THE CHURCH?

We will skin alive the priests? But why? We see that thousands of priests are now found in the vanguard of the movement and the contribution of the clergy which stood on our side, was invaluable. Is the opposite occurring? Why have those who claim to be defenders of the church killed, along with the Germans, so many priests and skinned some alive?

Communism will destroy religion. But religion is an issue of consciousness. How will it be destroyed? The destruction of religious consciousness is impossible even if the communists wanted to destroy it. Religious consciousness does not get destroyed by simple orders. If something like that occurred it would resemble the police officer in Anafi who disallowed the class struggle!

What will happen in the distant future: how will humans think is another problem. No politician can declare a law as to what should occur after 200 or 500 years. We won't produce such a law. We are interested in how the people will develop today and not what philosophical desires it has after 500 years.

Consequently do you understand that those who circulate such slander are aiming to achieve different ends, attempting with the method of slander to deceive the people and to maintain their dominance over them. If we analyse more deeply the issue we will see that they are non-religious as they have no religious consciousness. They only love God Mammon, the God of Money...

WE WILL MAKE THE FAMILY STRONGER

They also condemn the Communists, saying that they will dissolve families. As if we came down from the heavens and we weren't born in families but sprung up like mushrooms. The family was created by certain economic conditions. At a certain level of development of society the necessity of the family arose as because the demands of life were better served.

Everyone was required to work, the father and children on the farms the women stayed at home as that is the only way society could manage their biological needs.

The forms of economic activities which dominated then made the bonds of its members even stronger. Today what is happening? Today's economic conditions do not lead to the closest working of the family but its exact opposite.

Here is one example. A man marries but the day after he leaves for the USA to be able to confront the needs of life and his family. Who dissolves the family in this case? The Communists or the economic conditions which Capitalism created?

Here we see clearly that they who condemn us as wanting to dissolve the family are none other than those who dissolve it in reality whilst we aim to solidify it. We will give to the people the economic measures so the family isn't dissolved to the four corners of the Earth.

They condemn us that we want to abolish borders and dissolve the State. But the State we build today no longer exists as they dissolved it. Who therefore is a patriot? They or us? Capital doesn't have a country and it runs to find profit in whatever country it is able to. That is why it isn't concerned for the existence of borders and the state. But all we own are our hats and the small kerb in front of us, unlike capital that runs wherever it finds profit.

Who can be interested more in their country? They who remove the capital from this country or us who are stuck on our doorsteps here? When suddenly in 1929-31 the state asked due to the economic crisis which affected our country the foreign bond holders to lower the interest rates which we pay for the bonds, the English agreed to reduce it by 35% but the Greek bondholders refused. There is their patriotism! They reach to the point when their economic interests aren't affected. They themselves condemn us that we seek to abolish borders and the dissolution of the state, they sell everything out at every available opportunity.

WHEN DISHONORABLE PEOPLE SPEAK OF HONOUR.

They condemn us that we are the ones who oversee honour. They are all the moral persons who when they walk get their heads woven into the barbed wire, they speak of honour!

They who sold their women and sisters to the occupier, so as to do business with them and turned us into double slaves, they now go to convince us that they are the vanguard of honour and morality. With such means they are trying to deceive the people so as to continue the exploitation and torture. Many times they convince us and achieve what they say really is.

Take one example of what is going on the villages. The village smokes tobacco which he himself produces. But they convinced him that this is illegal. The villager himself then tells you that he is smoking illegal tobacco. As if he didn't grow it himself on his land but brought it from America. The villager himself ended up believing that his smoke was 'illegal'.

Reaction doesn't stop at anything so as to deceive the people, using all the means, all the sycophancy and lies. But these sycophancies in the country where they saw us and felt us became dust. The same will happen in the cities.

In a few days you will see reality yourselves alone. As our aim is only one: How our people will live better!

When the occupier was here they wanted order. We wanted disorder to make the life of the occupier unbearable. Now they disorder. We want order. They are the organisers of the civil war and they exploit our people. They are the wolves that try to eat the sheep you me us in other words the people.

WE MAINTAINED OUR PROMISES

EAM and ELAS promised to the people the struggle against the occupier and the liberation of the country. We maintain these promises. We didn't create a government press. It was created on its own by the people. From October 1942 the people on its own went for elections and their own self-government.

This institution of self-government which for the first time appeared in Evritania constituted its beginnings from creation in the village till the PEEA (govt of the mountains) later...

WE ARE FOR UNITY

We are for the unity and due to our attempts 95% of the creation of our national government under which we are fighting today. Until Larissa our country is now free. We will liberate the rest of the country soon.

Thus our second promise will be realised fully.

OUR STRUGGLE FOR POPULAR RULE

We also promised the people something else: that we won't leave our hands if we don't achieve our double freedom. That is what we will fight to achieve this promise of ours as well dedicating our lives and sacrificing it for a popular rule solution to the problems of the Greek problem.

ELAS in the first years of the CC of EAM and PEEA later constituted the strong weapon of maintaining the people in life. The vehicle of our faster liberation. Now in the hands of our national liberation which is composed by all the parties and organisations that support popular rule dominated solutions it will constitute a guarantee that we will continue the war until the full and complete victory of fascism and that they will guarantee the up till now gains of our people and more will be won.

You shouted a lot about the death penalty regarding the traitors and the collaborationists and exploiters of the people in the years of the occupation. When we didn't have the capacity of judging them we killed them. Later on we judged them in military tribunals. Now all those we have arrested we will hand over to justice. There exists now the legal government and this will decide for all. Don't shout therefore. They will be judged and condemned. It won't have a big importance. It will have great importance if you judge and condemn to death, the dominant people, the regime which creates such scumbags. Tomorrow we will go for elections. The first attack in the plebiscite must be the irrevocable condemnation of friendly royalism and the establishment of democracy.

WHY HAVE WE TURNED WITH SO MUCH HATRED AGAINST THE KING?

1. As first of all he isn't Greek.

2. They brought him here with the fake plebiscite of 1935.

3. As he is a person who disavowed his word. He squashed the constitution of 1911 and imposed the fifth-columnist Giannis Metaxas as dictator.

4. As he left all the incapable and fifth-columnist generals and ministers to betray us in the war in Albania and to subjugate the country.

5. Finally during our national disaster instead of staying here in 1941 to sacrifice himself as another Kodros of Athens he abandoned us.

If he was good he should have stayed here and instead of Aris Velouhiotis and I don't know who else going to the mountains he should have organised the struggle and to be by deed a King and our leader. With his stance he abandoned essentially and typically his right to be on the throne in Greece. That for sure for him personally and independently from our desires and that we don't need any throne, but democracy for Greece to go forward.

WE RESPECT THE POPULAR WILL

The second attack should be given to the elections which will clear the establishment of our country. As for us our only desire is that we become servants of the people. That is why we will respect your wishes whatever that may be.

But we have these demands: For the people to vote without influence and for them to respect the will of the people.

If these demands aren't carried out, then we promise you that we will go the mountains again. But I am sure these things won't happen. As our people have now got back their self-control. He was tried and woke up. He will follow the path which we show and which only interest him.

With this desire I ask you to shout:

LONG LIVE OUR DOMINANT PEOPLE!

How the IMF Dismantled Yugoslavia

by Michel Chossudovsky

[AUTHOR'S NOTE: A more detailed version of this article is contained in "The Globalization of Poverty, Impacts of IMF and World Bank Reforms" (1997, Zed Books). Macro-economic reforms imposed by Belgrade's external creditors since the late 1980s had been carefully synchronized with NATO's military and intelligence operations. Resulting from the IMF's deadly economic medicine, the entire Yugoslav economy had been spearheaded into bankruptcy.

In Kosovo, the economic reforms were conducive to the concurrent impoverishment of both the Albanian and Serbian populations contributing to fuelling ethnic tensions. The deliberate manipulation of market forces destroyed economic activity and people's livelihood creating a situation of social despair. In parallel with the destruction of federal Yugoslavia, similar macro-economic reforms under IMF auspices were imposed on Albania with devastating economic and social consequences.]

As heavily-armed U.S. and NATO troops enforce the peace in Bosnia, the press and politicians alike portray Western intervention in the former Yugoslavia as a noble, if agonizingly belated, response to an outbreak of ethnic massacres and human rights violations. In the wake of the November 1995 Dayton peace accords, the West is eager to touch up its self-portrait as savior of the Southern Slavs and get on with "the work of rebuilding" the newly sovereign states.

But following a pattern set early on, Western public opinion has been misled. The conventional wisdom holds that the plight of the Balkans is the outcome of an "aggressive nationalism", the inevitable result of deep-seated ethnic and religious tensions rooted in history. Likewise, commentators cite "Balkans power- plays" and the clash of political personalities to explain the conflicts.

Lost in the barrage of images and self-serving analyses are the economic and social causes of the conflict. The deep-seated economic crisis which preceded the civil war is long forgotten.

The strategic interests of Germany and the U.S. in laying the groundwork for the disintegration of Yugoslavia go unmentioned, as does the role of external creditors and international financial institutions. In the eyes of the global media, Western powers bear no responsibility for the impoverishment and destruction of a nation of 24 million people.

But through their domination of the global financial system, the Western powers, in pursuit of national and collective strategic interests, helped bring the Yugoslav economy to its knees and stirred simmering ethnic and social conflicts. Now it is the turn of Yugoslavia's war-ravaged successor states to feel the tender mercies of the international financial community.

As the world focuses on troop movements and cease fires, the international financial institutions are busily collecting former Yugoslavia's external debt from its remnant states, while transforming the Balkans into a safe-haven for free enterprise. With a Bosnian peace settlement holding under NATO guns, the West has unveiled a "reconstruction" program that strips that brutalized country of sovereignty to a degree not seen in Europe since the end of World War II. It consists largely of making Bosnia a divided territory under NATO military occupation and Western administration.

The reins of economic policy handed to the IMF

NEO-COLONIAL BOSNIA

Resting on the Dayton accords, which created a Bosnian "constitution," the US and the European Union have installed a full-fledged colonial administration in Bosnia. At its head is their appointed High Representative, Carl Bildt, a former Swedish prime minister and European Union representative in Bosnian peace negotiations. Bildt has full executive powers in all civilian matters, with the right to overrule the governments of both the Bosnian Federation and the Republika Srpska. To make the point crystal clear, the accords spell out that "The High Representative is the final authority in theater regarding interpretation of the agreements." He will work with IFOR's Military High Command as well as creditors and donors. The UN Security Council has also appointed a "commissioner" under the High Representative to run an international civilian police force. Irish police official Peter Fitzgerald, with previous UN policing experience in Namibia, El Salvador, and Cambodia, presides over some 1,700 policemen from 15 countries. The police will be dispatched to Bosnia after a five-day training program in Zagreb.

The new constitution hands the reins of economic policy over to the Bretton Woods institutions and the London-based European Bank for Reconstruction and Development (EBRD). The IMF is empowered to appoint the first governor of the Bosnian Central Bank, who, like the High Representative, "shall not be a citizen of Bosnia and Herzegovina or a neighboring State."

Under the IMF regency, the Central Bank will not be allowed to function as a Central Bank: "For the first six years . . . it may not extend credit by creating money, operating in this respect as a currency board." Neither will Bosnia be allowed to have its own currency (issuing paper money only when there is full foreign exchange backing), nor permitted to mobilize its internal resources. Its ability to self-finance its reconstruction through an independent monetary policy is blunted from the outset.

While the Central Bank is in IMF custody, the European Bank for Reconstruction and Development (EBRD) heads the Commission on Public Corporations, which supervises operations of all public sector corporations, including energy, water, postal services, telecommunications, and transportation. The EBRD president appoints the commission's chair and will direct public sector restructuring, meaning primarily the sell-off of state and socially-owned assets and the procurement of long term investment funds. Western creditors explicitly created the EBRD "to give a distinctively political dimension to lending."

As the West trumpets its support for democracy, actual political power rests in the hands of a parallel Bosnian "state" whose executive positions are held by non-citizens. Western creditors have embedded their interests in a constitution hastily written on their behalf. They have done so without a constitutional assembly, without consultations with Bosnian citizens' organizations and without providing a means of amending this "constitution." Their plans to rebuild Bosnia appear more suited to sating creditors than satisfying even the elementary needs of Bosnians.
And why not? The neo-colonization of Bosnia is the logical culmination of long Western efforts to undo Yugoslavia's experiment in market socialism and workers' self-management and impose in its place the diktat of the free market.

Yugoslavia's implosion was in part due to U.S. machinations during the Reagan years

THE SHAPE OF THINGS TO COME

Multi-ethnic, socialist Yugoslavia was once a regional industrial power and economic success. In the two decades prior to 1980, annual GDP growth averaged 6.1 percent, medical care was free, the literacy rate was of the order of 91 percent, and the life expectancy was 72 years. But after a decade of Western economic ministrations and five years of disintegration, war, boycott, and embargo, the economies of the former Yugoslavia are prostrate, their industrial sectors dismantled. Yugoslavia's implosion was in part due to U.S. machinations. Despite Belgrade's non-alignment and its extensive trading relations with the European Community and the U.S., the Reagan administration targeted the Yugoslav economy in a "Secret Sensitive" 1984 National Security Decision Directive (NSDD 133), "United States Policy toward Yugoslavia." A censored version declassified in 1990 largely elaborated on NSDD 54 on Eastern Europe, issued in 1982. The latter advocated "expanded efforts to promote a 'quiet revolution' to overthrow Communist governments and parties" while reintegrating the countries of Eastern Europe into a market-oriented economy.

The U.S. had earlier joined Belgrade's other international creditors in imposing a first round of macroeconomic reform in 1980, shortly before the death of Marshall Tito. Successive IMF- sponsored programs since then continued the disintegration of the industrial sector and the piecemeal dismantling of the Yugoslav welfare state. Debt restructuring agreements increased foreign debt, and a mandated currency devaluation also hit hard at Yugoslavs' standard of living.

This initial round of restructuring set the pattern. Throughout the 1980s, the IMF prescribed further doses of its bitter economic medicine periodically as the Yugoslav economy slowly lapsed into a coma. Industrial production declined to a negative 10 percent growth rate by 1990 -- with all its predictable social consequences.

By cutting the financial arteries between Belgrade and the republics, the reforms fuelled secession

MR. MARKOVIC GOES TO WASHINGTON

In autumn 1989, just before the fall of the Berlin Wall, Yugoslav federal Premier Ante Markovic met in Washington with President George Bush to cap negotiations for a new financial aid package. In return for assistance, Yugoslavia agreed to even more sweeping economic reforms, including a new devalued currency, another wage freeze, sharp cuts in government spending, and the elimination of socially-owned, worker-managed companies. The Belgrade nomenklatura, with the assistance of Western advisers, had laid the groundwork for the prime minister's mission by implementing beforehand many of the required reforms, including a major liberalization of foreign investment legislation. "Shock therapy" began in January 1990. Although inflation had eaten away at earnings, the IMF ordered that wages be frozen at their mid-November 1989 level. Prices continued to rise unabated, and real wages collapsed by 41 percent in the first six months of 1990.

The IMF also effectively controlled the Yugoslav central bank. Its tight money policy further crippled federal Yugoslavia's ability to finance its economic and social programs. State revenues that should have gone as transfer payments to the republics and provinces went instead to service Belgrade's debt with the Paris and London clubs. The republics were largely left to their own devices.

In one fell swoop, the reformers engineered the final collapse of Yugoslavia's federal fiscal structure and mortally wounded its federal political institutions. By cutting the financial arteries between Belgrade and the republics, the reforms fueled secessionist tendencies that fed on economic factors as well as ethnic divisions and virtually ensured the de facto secession of the republics. The IMF-induced budgetary crisis created an economic fait accompli that paved the way for Croatia's and Slovenia's formal secession in June 1991.

The dismantling of the industrial economy was breath-taking in its magnitude and brutality

CRUSHED BY THE INVISIBLE HAND

The reforms demanded by Belgrade's creditors also struck at the heart of Yugoslavia's system of socially-owned and worker-managed enterprises. As one observer noted, "The objective was to subject the Yugoslav economy to massive privatization and the dismantling of the public sector. The Communist Party bureaucracy, most notably its military and intelligence sector, was canvassed specifically and offered political and economic backing on the condition that wholesale scuttling of social protections for Yugoslavia's workforce was imposed." It was an offer that a desperate Yugoslavia could not refuse. Advised by Western lawyers and consultants, Markovic's government passed financial legislation that forced "insolvent" businesses into bankruptcy or liquidation. Under the new law, if a business were unable to pay its bills for 30 days running, or for 30 days within a 45-day period, the government would launch bankruptcy procedures within the next 15 days.

The assault on the socialist economy also included a new banking law designed to trigger the liquidation of the socially owned "Associated Banks." Within two years, more than half the country's banks had vanished, to be replaced by newly-formed "independent profit-oriented institutions."

These changes in the legal framework, combined with the IMF's tight money policy toward industry and the opening of the economy to foreign competition, accelerated industrial decline. >From 1989 through September 1990, more than a thousand companies went into bankruptcy. By 1990, the annual rate of growth of GDP had collapsed to -7.5 percent. In 1991, GDP declined by a further 15 percent, while industrial output shrank by 21 percent.

The IMF package unquestionably precipitated the collapse of much of Yugoslavia's well-developed heavy industry. Other socially-owned enterprises survived only by not paying workers. More than half a million workers still on company payrolls did not get regular paychecks in late 1990. They were the lucky ones. Some 600,000 Yugoslavs had already lost their jobs by September 1990, and that was only the beginning. According to the World Bank, another 2,435 industrial enterprises, including some of the country's largest, were slated for liquidation. Their 1.3 million workers -- half the remaining industrial workforce -- were "redundant."

As 1991 dawned, real wages were in free fall, social programs had collapsed, and unemployment ran rampant. The dismantling of the industrial economy was breath-taking in its magnitude and brutality. Its social and political impact, while not as easily quantified, was tremendous. "The pips are squeaking," as London's patrician Financial Times put it.

Less archly, Yugoslav President Borisav Jovic warned that the reforms were "having a markedly unfavourable impact on the overall situation in society . . . Citizens have lost faith in the state and its institutions . . . The further deepening of the economic crisis and the growth of social tensions has had a vital impact on the deterioration of the political-security situation."

With the republics at each others' throats, both economy and the nation itself embarked on a vicious downward spiral

THE POLITICAL ECONOMY OF DISINTEGRATION

Some Yugoslavs joined together in a doomed battle to prevent the destruction of their economy and polity. As one observer found, "worker resistance crossed ethnic lines, as Serbs, Croats, Bosnians and Slovenians mobilized . . . shoulder to shoulder with their fellow workers." But the economic struggle also heightened already tense relations among the republics -- and between the republics and Belgrade. Serbia rejected the austerity plan outright, and some 650,000 Serbian workers struck against the federal government to force wage hikes. The other republics followed different and sometimes self-contradictory paths.

In relatively wealthy Slovenia, for instance, secessionist leaders such as Social Democratic party chair Joze Pucnik supported the reforms: "From an economic standpoint, I can only agree with socially harmful measures in our society, such as rising unemployment or cutting workers' rights, because they are necessary to advance the economic reform process."
But at the same time, Slovenia joined other republics in challenging the federal government's efforts to restrict their economic autonomy. Both Croatian leader Franjo Tudjman and Serbia's Slobodan Milosevic joined Slovene leaders in railing against Yugoslavia's attempts to impose harsh reforms.

In the multi-party elections in 1990, economic policy was at the center of the political debate as separatist coalitions ousted the Communists in Croatia, Bosnia and Slovenia. Just as economic collapse spurred the drift toward separation, the separation in turn exacerbated the economic crisis. Cooperation among the republics virtually ceased. And with the republics at each others' throats, both economy and the nation itself embarked on a vicious downward spiral.

The process sped downward as the republican leaderships deliberately fostered social and economic divisions to strengthen their own hands: "The republican oligarchies, who all had visions of a 'national renaissance' of their own, instead of choosing between a genuine Yugoslav market and hyperinflation, opted for war which would disguise the real causes of the economic catastrophe." The simultaneous appearance of militias loyal to secessionist leaders only hastened the descent into chaos. These militias, with their escalating atrocities, not only split the population along ethnic lines, they also fragmented the workers' movement.

Slovenia, Croatia, and finally, Bosnia fought bloody civil wars

WESTERN HELP

The austerity measures had laid the basis for the recolonization of the Balkans. Whether that required the breakup of Yugoslavia was subject to debate among the Western powers, with Germany leading the push for secession and the U.S., fearful of opening a nationalist pandora's box, originally arguing for Yugoslavia's preservation. Following Franjo Tudjman's and the rightist Democratic Union's decisive victory in Croatia in May 1990, German Foreign Minister Hans Dietrich Genscher, in almost daily contacts with his counterpart in Zagreb, gave his go-ahead for Croatian secession. Germany did not passively support secession; it "forced the pace of international diplomacy" and pressured its Western allies to recognize Slovenia and Croatia. Germany sought a free hand among its allies "to pursue economic dominance in the whole of Mitteleuropa."

Washington, on the other hand, favored "a loose unity while encouraging democratic development . . . [Secretary of State] Baker told Tudjman and [Slovenia's President] Milan Kucan that the United States would not encourage or support unilateral secession . . . but if they had to leave, he urged them to leave by a negotiated agreement."

Instead, Slovenia, Croatia, and finally, Bosnia fought bloody civil wars against "rump" Yugoslavia (Serbia and Montenegro) or Serbian nationalists or both. But now, the U.S. has belatedly taken an active diplomatic role in Bosnia, strengthened its relations with Croatia, and Macedonia, and positioned itself to play a leading role in the region's economic and political future.

Yugoslavia's foreign debt has been carefully divided among the successor republics, which are now strangled in making separate arrangements

THE POST-WAR REGIME

Western creditors have now turned their attention to Yugoslavia's successor states. As with the demise of Yugoslavia, the economic aspects of post-war reconstruction remain largely unheralded, but the prospects for rebuilding the newly independent republics appear bleak. Yugoslavia's foreign debt has been carefully divided and allocated to the successor republics, which are now strangled in separate debt rescheduling and structural adjustment agreements. The consensus among donors and international agencies is that past macroeconomic reforms adopted under IMF advice had not quite met their goal and further shock therapy is required to restore "economic health" in Yugoslavia's successor states. Croatia and Macedonia have followed the IMF's direction. Both have agreed to loan packages -- to pay off their shares of the Yugoslav debt -- which require a consolidation of the process begun with Ante Markovic's bankruptcy program. The too familiar pattern of plant closings, induced bank failures, and impoverishment continues apace.

And global capital applauds. Despite an emerging crisis in social welfare and the decimation of his economy, Macedonian Finance Minister Ljube Trpevski proudly informed the press that "the World Bank and the IMF place Macedonia among the most successful countries in regard to current transition reforms."

The head of the IMF mission to Macedonia, Paul Thomsen, agreed.

He avowed that "the results of the stabilization program were impressive" and gave particular credit to "the efficient wages policy" adopted by the Skopje government. Still, his negotiators added, even more budget cutting will be necessary'
.

But Western intervention is making its most serious inroads on national sovereignty in Bosnia. The neo-colonial administration imposed by the Dayton accords, supported by NATO's firepower, ensures that Bosnia's future will be determined in Washington, Bonn, and Brussels -- not Sarajevo.

"Substantial" petroleum fields also lie in the Serb-held part of Croatia

RECONSTRUCTION COLONIAL STYLE

If Bosnia is ever to emerge from the ravages of war and neo-colonialism, massive reconstruction will be essential. But judging by recent Balkan history, Western assistance is more likely to drag Bosnia into the Third World rather than lift it to parity with its European neighbors. The Bosnian government estimates that reconstruction costs will reach $47 billion. Western donors have pledged $3 billion in reconstruction loans, yet only $518 million dollars have so far been granted. Part of this money is tagged to finance some of the local civilian costs of IFOR's military deployment and part to repay international creditors.

Fresh loans will pay back old debt. The Central Bank of the Netherlands has generously provided "bridge financing" of $37 million to allow Bosnia to pay its arrears with the IMF, without which the IMF will not lend it fresh money. But in a cruel and absurd paradox, the sought-after loans from the IMF's newly created "Emergency Window" for "post-conflict countries" will not be used for post-war reconstruction. Instead, they will repay the Dutch Central Bank, which had coughed up the money to settle IMF arrears in the first place. Debt piles up, and little new money goes for rebuilding Bosnia's war-torn economy.

While rebuilding is sacrificed on the altar of debt repayment, Western governments and corporations show greater interest in gaining access to strategic natural resources. With the discovery of energy reserves in the region, the partition of Bosnia between the Federation of Bosnia-Herzegovina and the Bosnian-Serb Republika Srpska under the Dayton accords has taken on new strategic importance. Documents in the hands of Croatia and the Bosnian Serbs indicate that coal and oil deposits have been identified on the eastern slope of the Dinarides Thrust, retaken from rebel Krajina Serbs by the US-backed Croatian army in the final offensives before the Dayton accords. Bosnian officials report that Chicago-based Amoco was among several foreign firms that subsequently initiated exploratory surveys in Bosnia.

"Substantial" petroleum fields also lie in the Serb-held part of Croatia just across the Sava river from Tuzla, the headquarters for the U.S. military zone. Exploration operations went on during the war, but the World Bank and the multinationals which conducted the operations kept local governments in the dark, presumably to prevent them from acting to grab potentially valuable areas.

With their attention devoted to debt repayment and potential energy bonanzas, the Western powers have shown little interest in rectifying the crimes committed under the rubric of ethnic cleansing. The 70,000 NATO troops on hand to "enforce the peace" will accordingly devote their efforts to administering the partition of Bosnia in accordance with Western economic interests rather than restoring the status quo ante.

While local leaders and Western interests share the spoils of the former Yugoslav economy, they have entrenched socio-ethnic divisions in the very structure of partition. This permanent fragmentation of Yugoslavia along ethnic lines serves to thwart a united resistance of Yugoslavs of all ethnic origins against the recolonization of their homeland.

But what's new? As one observer caustically noted, all of the leaders of Yugoslavia's successor states have worked closely with the West: "All the current leaders of the former Yugoslav republics were Communist Party functionaires and each in turn vied to meet the demands of the World Bank and the International Monetary Fund, the better to qualify for investment loans and substantial perks for the leadership."

A world of shuttered factories, jobless workers, and gutted social programs Western-backed neo-liberal macroeconomic restructuring helped destroy Yugoslavia. Yet, since the onset of war in 1991, the global media has carefully overlooked or denied its central role. Instead, it has joined the chorus singing praises of the free market as the basis for rebuilding a war-shattered economy. The social and political impact of economic restructuring in Yugoslavia has been carefully erased from our collective understanding. Opinion-makers instead dogmatically present cultural, ethnic, and religious divisions as the sole cause of the crisis. In reality, they are the consequence of a much deeper process of economic and political fracturing. This false consciousness not only masks the truth, it also prevents us from acknowledging precise historical occurrences.

Ultimately it distorts the true sources of social conflict. When applied to the former Yugoslavia, it obscures the historical foundations of South Slavic unity, solidarity and identity. But this false consciousness lives worldwide, where the only possible world is one of shuttered factories, jobless workers, and gutted social programs, and "bitter economic medicine" is the only prescription.

At stake in the Balkans are the lives of millions of people. Macroeconomic reform there has destroyed livelihoods and made a joke of the right to work. It has put basic needs such as food and shelter beyond the reach of many. It has degraded culture and national identity. In the name of global capital, borders have been redrawn, legal codes rewritten, industries destroyed, financial and banking systems dismantled, social programs eliminated. No alternative to global capital, be it market socialism or "national" capitalism, will be allowed to exist.

But what happened to Yugoslavia -- and now continues in its weak successor states -- should resonate beyond the Balkans. Yugoslavia is a mirror for similar economic restructuring programs in not only the developing world but also in the US, Canada and Western Europe. The Yugoslav reforms are the cruel reflection of a destructive economic model pushed to the extreme.

By Way of an ….Epilogue

The articles which were included in this book were written essentially from May 2010-till July 2011 i.e. the first phase of the rapacious IMF measures. Since then we have had another couple of General Strikes, schools have opened for the first time since 1974 without the Government printing textbooks alongside school children collapsing in class without having eaten and there have been many strikes in almost as many sections of workers as before, due to the proposed cuts in wages (around 30% for public sector employees) and the newly proposed property tax which will range from a few hundred to a few thousand Euros annually alongside the abolition of all nationally agreed collective wage agreements. In other words a return to an era of open direct slavery, a new barbarism in an era with the technological advancements we have we could less work, but work for all.

The sold out union barons, the political parties of the fake Left, continue their disunited campaign of controlled resistance. In the demonstrations and strikes of June only a small unorganised minority called for the people to occupy Parliament and remain in Sindagma Sq., but the vast majority were still unconscious of the period we are living through. They weren't as yet willing to rebel to overthrow the political system despite the dynamic of the slogans. Most people as yet believed that the start of the IMF measures would eventually give way to a new economic upturn or the measures would eventually be put on hold and possibly work by stabilising the situation.

The supranational economic elite having knowledge the impasse they are in, due to the economic crisis and the measures they are taking and what their effect will be, are trying to forestall an insurrection by taking pre-emptive measures on a multitude of fronts. They have experience in being able to provoke pre-emptive rebellions that they can then put down, they can provoke resistance to see how to combat it by preparing their personnel and as such some of the events of the last 16 months contain all of these features from the provocation-murder of the bank workers, to the local insurrection in Keratea and the mass media sponsored surrounding of Parliament from all sides. Frequent media referrals to an army intervention also play the role of instilling fear in the protestors.

The secret state organised the calling of the Greek Indignants to the squares, but hundreds of thousands of course came out of their own free will. What did the state achieve with this?

Three elements:
1. Solidifying the hardline sections of the riot police to confront people in a manner akin to previous eras as the demonstrators started out initially in a jovial manner way back in May and by the end of June, both sides had hardened their stance significantly. As a riot copper said in a lull in the fighting 'as yet you don't have the balls or courage to do us and we as yet don't have the same to send you all underground'...

2. They organised all the known state provocateurs in the bottom half of the square to be ready at any moment in time to create provocations with the police so they can attack the mass disorganised peaceful crowds in order to instill fear in society as a whole.

3. The provisionally depressed the masses by endless speeches and not organisation to create self-defence units and prepare for the riot police attacks with something more than plastic water bottles and gas masks. The top end of the square – the most militant – didn't break out of its sloganeering and organise itself to take leadership of the whole square and thus let the bottom end of the square – where the fake left globalists dominate – to run the show.

One must take into account the above when having read this book, as the state is a player in events in more ways than one can imagine and what appears to be happening, may not indeed be happening at all. That does not imply that they are totally in control. They are trying their best, but they will lose control and they are playing with fire. Necessity is the mother of invention and the Greek nation will find the means and ways to survive. It has to, otherwise it will be erased from it's 5,000 year history. This is a small contribution to all those who are working for that goal.

VN Gelis

Postscript:
Special thanks to DK Lawrence who helped in the editing of the book and without whom this would have proven much harder in producing than it was.

Political Parties:

PASOK-Pan-Hellenic Socialist Movement led by Papandreou

New Democracy led by Samaras

KKE led by Papariga

Laos led by Karatzaferis

Sinaspismos led by Alavanos

Dimokratiki Aristera led by Kouvelis

Websites mentioned in this book:

Greek ones:

www.kke.gr

http://patari.org/

http://imfoccupationgreece.blogspot.com/

British ones

http://www.permanentrevolution.net/

http://www.cpgb.org.uk/worker/

www.ingramcontent.com/pod-product-compliance
Lightning Source LLC
Chambersburg PA
CBHW060247290526
45789CB00001B/232